International Financial Liberalization:

The Impact on World Development

John Eatwell

United Nations Development Programme
Office of Development Studies
Discussion Paper Series

Contents

Foreword v

Executive Summary 1

1. Introduction 3

2. Assessing the Experience of Liberalization 9
   - Criteria for Evaluation 9
   - Comparing Reality with Expectations 12

3. Explaining the Record of Liberalization 27
   - Financial Markets and the Real Economy 27
   - How Market Views Are Formed 30
   - Consequences for Public Policy 32

4. Liberal Financial Markets and the Private Sector 37
   - Developed Economies 38
   - Emerging Markets 43

5. Conclusions 46

Notes 51

Bibliography 58

Author's Biographical Note 66

I am grateful to Sara Sawhney for research assistance. I am also indebted to Edward Amadeo, Barry Eichengreen, Ricardo Ffrench-Davis, Tony Porter, Ajit Singh, Paul Streeten and Charles Wyplosz, who provided a number of incisive criticisms which I have done my best to take into account.

Foreword

The 1990's have been a period of excitement and apprehension for developing countries, especially when it comes to decisions to lift controls on the movements of money flowing in and out of their economies. Chastised by the experience of the Mexican crisis in 1994, they are nevertheless encouraged by the record of other developing countries in Latin America and Asia, that have successfully attracted foreign capital. In order to weigh the risks and benefits of decisions that involve financial liberalization, policy-makers in developing countries need to form an opinion on whether or not past experiences have validated the claims of the proponents of liberalization.

In this Discussion Paper, John Eatwell proposes to test these claims by examining the record of the past thirty years in a sample of countries for which relevant data is most available. Indeed, the years from 1965 until now have witnessed a systemic change, from an era when both governments and international organizations devoted energy to the tight management of financial phenomena, to one where this political energy is spent in experimenting with liberalization in the hope of faster development.

Eatwell finds surprising evidence that liberalization, when it has occurred, has not yielded results that conform to standard expectations. He also raises disturbing questions on the possibility that some aspects of liberalization may thwart, rather than promote, growth and development. In conclusion, he urges serious consideration of alternative approaches, and in particular a more pragmatic approach to liberalization strategies.

While his views are those of an independent scholar and do not represent those of UNDP or its Office of Development Studies, we hope that this paper will promote a healthy exchange of ideas and arguments on this topical issue. In particular, we would like to encourage responses from policy-makers and economists in the South on the general points made here, and on the extent to which the paper's conclusions tally with the recent experiences of particular developing countries. Further work is also needed on sub-national phenomena, in particular gender-specific studies, or studies of the impact of financial liberalization on specific income groups.

We invite readers to send us their comments on this Discussion paper, which we will be happy to consider publishing in a companion volume.

It is only in such an atmosphere of free examination of data and evidence and professional debate, that policy-makers can hope to make enlightened decisions in the interest of sustainable human development.

Inge Kaul
Director
Office of Development Studies
New York, September 1996

Executive Summary

The widespread liberalization of international financial flows followed the end of the Bretton Woods system of fixed parities among the world's major currencies. The trend toward openness has accelerated in the 1980's and 1990's, encouraging the creation of a global, $1250 billion dollar a day foreign exchange market, and stimulating the invention of many new financial instruments. Liberalization is now spreading rapidly to emerging economies. Yet it is not clear that the optimism that underpins this global liberalization effort is warranted.

An examination of the record of financial liberalization reveals that many hoped for benefits have failed to materialize. First, liberalization was expected to improve the allocation of global capital by moving resources from capital-rich to capital-poor countries. In fact, the record shows that *net* financial flows (and their counterpart flows of real resources) have been very modest, and predominantly *toward* the capital-rich. Second, liberalization was supposed to enhance opportunities for savers and lower costs to borrowers. In fact, the rewards accrued mostly to savers, in the form of the highest real interest rates in modern times. Third, the wider development of derivatives, which was supposed to improve risk management, created new systemic risks of its own. Fourth, the improved macro-economic performance that was expected in the form of higher investment and growth due to better allocative efficiency, failed to materialize. On the contrary, overall performance has been inferior to what was achieved in the pre-liberalization period. Finally, financial liberalization was supposed to bring to bear a "healthy discipline" on individual governments, improving macro-economic stability. In fact, liberalization has imposed a persistent deflationary bias on economic policy, as governments attempt to secure "credibility" in the hope of averting destabilizing capital flows.

A variety of factors may be to blame for the disappointing performance of the post-Bretton Woods global economy. But the impact of financial liberalization, and the potential scale of capital flows today, is an important component of any global explanation.

Why should free international capital flows be associated with a deterioration in economic efficiency (as measured by growth and employment)? Essentially because financial markets do not merely process the financial information necessary to secure an efficient allocation of real resources. Instead, they tend to operate in such a way that their own "beliefs" are imposed on the real economy, becoming self-fulfilling prophecies. The markets create their own "fundamentals." If the markets *expect* reduced unemployment or higher fiscal deficits to raise interest rates, then higher interest rates will indeed follow. Moreover, the potential for instability in today's massive capital markets induces both governments and private-sector investors in the real economy to pursue highly risk-averse strategies. The result is low growth and high unemployment. However, given the theory of economic policy that dominates official thinking today, it is unlikely that a significant reassertion of control over international financial structures is possible without an equally major change in priorities and analyses by all governments in developed and developing countries alike.

1.
Introduction

The impact of the liberalization of international financial markets on the scale of cross-border capital flows has become an increasingly familiar tale. Yet the extraordinary growth of international capital flows in recent years makes it a tale worthy of retelling. It is the product of the most important systemic transformation of the world economy since the establishment of the new world order at the end of World War II. The current and potential impact of the explosion in international capital flows on the organization and operation of developed and developing economies demands detailed evaluation. It is the key to the world's economic future.

The Scale of Capital Flows

In 1973 daily foreign exchange trading around the world varied between $10 billion and $20 billion per day. On 1st January 1974, the United States abolished all restrictions on international capital movements, following the same move by Canada, Germany and Switzerland during 1973. Britain scrapped all controls in 1979, Japan in 1980, France and Italy in 1990, and Spain and Portugal in 1992.

Following the abolition of controls the volume of international capital flows has grown exponentially. During the 1970s foreign exchange trading led the way. By 1980, according to the Bank for International Settlements (BIS) (1993), foreign exchange trading had reached a daily average of $80 billion, and the ratio of foreign exchange trading to world trade was about 10/1. By 1992, daily trading averaged $880 billion, a ratio to world trade of 50/1. In 1995 daily trading averaged $1260 billion, a ratio to world trade of nearly 70/1, equal to the entire world's official gold and foreign exchange reserves (BIS, 1996). These figures are for an *average* day's trading and will be greatly exceeded on days of high activity, such as the days of September 1992 when the pound sterling was forced out of the European Exchange Rate Mechanism (ERM) and the French franc was under sustained speculative attack. As is clear from Table 1, by far the greatest part of currency trades was very short run. Given that the vast majority of trades are not for the finance of trade in goods or services or long term investment, these short term trades must be based on expectations of gain derived from changes in the value of financial assets. In the broadest sense, they are speculative.[1]

In the 1980s it was the turn of the international bond markets. From 1983 to 1993 total cross-border (cross-currency) sales and purchases of United States Treasury bonds rose from $30 billion to $500 billion. Sales and purchases of bonds and equities between foreigners and United States residents rose from 3% of United States GDP in 1970 to 9% in 1980, to 135% in 1993. Over the same period, cross-border securities transactions in the United Kingdom rose from "virtually nothing" to more than 1000%

Table 1. Maturity of Net Global foreign exchange transactions, April 1992 and April 1995 (percentages)

	Spot[a]	.... Forward[b]		
	$x \leq 2$	$2 < x \leq 7$	$7 < x \leq 365$	$365 < x$
1992	47.3	33.9	18.2	0.6
1995	43.5	38.1	17.5	0.8

x = number of days maturity

Note: a. Single outright currency exchanges with cash settlements within two business days. Excludes the spot leg of swaps. b. Swaps, outright forwards traded on exchanges or "customized" and currency options at their notional value. Cross-currency swaps of interest and amortization instalments not included.
Sources: BIS (1993), BIS (1996).

of GDP. Woodall (1995) cites an IMF estimate that "total cross-border ownership of tradable securities in 1992 was $2,500 billion."

The growth in trading has been accompanied by a growth in the stock of international bank lending, from $265 billion in 1975 to $4200 billion in 1994. The McKinsey Global Institute estimates that the total stock of all financial assets traded in global (i.e. open) markets rose from $5,000 billion in 1980 to $35,000 billion in 1992, equal to twice the GDP of the OECD countries. By 2000, McKinsey forecasts that the stock of globally traded assets will have reached $83,000 billion, about three times OECD GDP (Woodall, 1995).

It is no accident that the explosive growth of international capital flows coincided with the 1973 collapse of the Bretton Woods system of fixed exchange rates. Apart from comparatively rare realignments, fixed rates offered only the profits of limited arbitrage. The fluctuating rate system that took its place stimulated capital flows with a powerful cocktail of the carrot of speculative profit and the stick of financial risk, laced with the proceeds of extensive arbitrage.

To an important extent, profit-seeking speculation is an inevitable outcome of the abandonment of fixed rates. Under the Bretton Woods system, there was little profit to be had in speculation, since currencies moved only in very tight bands, apart, that is, from the very occasional change in parity. Indeed, the Bretton Woods system provided quite remarkable stability. For example, the core currencies of the European Monetary System, locked together in the 1980s in the ERM, were *less* stable in relation to one another than they had been during the 1950s and 1960s. In the face of Bretton Woods stability it was not worthwhile creating the infrastructure of large scale currency dealing facilities with which we are familiar today—even if the contemporary regulatory structures had not placed significant barriers in the path of capital flows. Nonetheless, in the 1960s growing speculative capital flows and the consequent pressure on fixed parities, notably the dollar price of gold, played a large part in the demise of the Bretton Woods system (Triffin, 1960; Black 1987; De Grauwe, 1987). But once Bretton Woods had collapsed and significant fluctuations in exchange rates became commonplace, then opportunities for profit proliferated, regulatory structures which inhibit flows of capital were challenged as "inefficient" and "against the national interest," and the modern infrastructure of speculation was constructed.

The incentive to deregulate international capital flows was powerfully reinforced by the need to hedge against the costs that fluctuating exchange rates imposed upon the private sector. Under the Bretton Woods system, foreign exchange risk was borne by the public sector. With that system's collapse, foreign exchange risk was privatized.

This privatization of risk imposed substantial strains on the domestic and international banking systems. The need to absorb and cover foreign exchange risk demanded the creation of new financial instruments, which in turn required the removal of many of the regulatory barriers which limited the possibilities of laying off risk, and a restructuring of financial institutions. Combined with other domestic pressures for the removal of financial controls, the collapse of Bretton Woods was a significant factor driving the world-wide deregulation of financial systems. Exchange controls were abolished. Domestic restrictions on cross-market access for financial institutions were scrapped. Quantitative controls on the growth of credit were eliminated, and monetary policy was now conducted predominantly through the management of short-term interest rates. A global market in monetary instruments was created.

The "Official" Position on Capital Controls

With the appearance of the new global financial market came an equally fundamental shift in the official assessment of the value of capital controls.

The liberalization of international capital movements was not one of the objectives of the 1944 Articles of Agreement which established the International Monetary Fund (IMF). The goal of convertibility was associated with current account transactions alone. Indeed, debate at the Bretton Woods conference revolved around whether Article VI of the Articles of Agreement should not merely permit the imposition of capital controls but also should *require* the IMF and other countries to assist in the enforcement of any member's controls against capital flight. This had been Keynes's objective from the first draft of his plan for a Clearing Union. In due course, pressure from the US Department, the Federal Reserve Bank of New York, and Wall Street bankers resulted in the adoption of the compromise embodied in Article VI.[2] Under that Article, member states are allowed to impose permanent controls and the IMF is required to ensure that its credits are not used to fund capital flight, but neither the

Fund nor other countries have any obligation to assist in the enforcement of a country's capital controls.

The IMF's practice today is exactly the opposite of both the letter and the intent of Article VI. Not only is IMF lending now conditional on measures which enhance the attractiveness of borrowers to international investors (including the lifting of capital controls), but also IMF assistance has been provided explicitly to enable countries to withstand capital flight without imposing controls. The IMF reaction to the 1994 Mexican crisis is the most dramatic example of this approach. In order to eliminate the contradiction, the Fund's managing director, Michel Camdessus, has proposed that Article VI be revised. In its place would be a requirement that the currencies of all member countries be freely convertible for all capital transactions in order "to lock in the freedom of capital movements already achieved and encourage wider liberalization" (Camdessus, 1994).

The World Bank has also become active in the encouragement of capital market liberalization. Its affiliate, the International Finance Corporation, is fostering stock market development in developing countries and encouraging them to open their capital markets to foreign portfolio investment (Sudweeks, 1989). The encouragement of the growth of stock markets is a fundamental pillar of the World Bank's proposals for pension reform (World Bank, 1994; Singh, 1995).

The change in the practice of the Bretton Woods institutions reflects a change in the conventional wisdom. The experience of the Great Depression had led Keynes (1933, p. 236) to argue, "above all, let finance be primarily national," a view which was maintained in the Bretton Woods negotiations not only by Keynes but by White, too. Today, however, the belief that a freeing of capital flows would be "efficient," that it would bring about the convergence of long term interest rates and optimize the global allocation of capital, has been accepted by even the most careful commentators.[3] For example, in considering Richard Marston's demonstration (1993) that in Britain, Germany and the United States "capital controls imposed during the Bretton Woods period led to large covered interest differentials," Barry Eichengreen (1993, p. 626–627) comments: "Post-World War II capital controls were a potential source of allocational inefficiency. *Thus*, there was nothing particularly admirable about financial market performance under Bretton Woods" (emphasis added). Paul Krugman (1993, p. 540) is more equivocal: "The capital controls of the Bretton

Woods era may not have made a good deal of sense—but then the free capital flows of our own time do not make much sense either."

What is lacking on both sides of the argument are clear criteria for the evaluation of the impact of liberalization. In Section 2 of this Report, the impact of international financial liberalization is assessed in the light of an explicit list of claimed benefits. It is found that empirical evidence, with respect both to developed and developing countries, is not supportive of these claims. Section 3 contains an analysis which seems to accord more closely with the facts and an assessment of the impact on public policy, while Section 4 examines the impact of financial liberalization on the private sector of the real economy.

2.
Assessing the Experience of Liberalization

CRITERIA FOR EVALUATION

The argument that liberalization will enhance economic efficiency derives from some basic propositions in economic theory. Before turning to an examination of the facts, it may be useful to consider that theoretical framework, within which the experience of liberalization is typically presented.

Theoretical Arguments for the Efficiency of Liberalization

Implicit in virtually all arguments in favour of liberalization is the first part of the Fundamental Theorem of Welfare Economics (that competitive markets yield Pareto optimal equilibria) combined with the Efficient Market Hypothesis (that financial markets use information efficiently).

The argument that competitive markets are "efficient," and hence that capital controls are "inefficient," rests on the Fundamental Theorem, even though the concept of Pareto optimality has well-known limitations. A corollary of the same argument proposes that, in the absence of distortions, economies typically operate at or near full capacity, at the "natural rate of unemployment." The Fundamental Theorem presumes a perfectly competitive economy, with no externalities, in which consumer tastes are innate and the economy is always in equilibrium (Graaf, 1957). If these conditions do not hold, then the conclusions of the theorem do not hold. Nor is a partial fulfillment of these conditions necessarily superior to their total absence (Lipsey and Lancaster, 1956; Bohm, 1987). The associated Pareto criterion famously ignores all issues of distribution. An economy in which one individual is fabulously rich whilst others live in grinding poverty may be Pareto optimal.[4]

The Efficient Markets Hypothesis portrays financial markets as efficient gatherers and transmitters of information (Malkiel, 1987). When that information includes knowledge of the "true" behaviour of the economy ("the fundamentals"), then financial assets embody the true value of their real counterparts, creating an environment in which rational agents trading in these assets can make Pareto-efficient decisions. With rational expectations, agents do not make decisions about the future that are systematically proven to be wrong. Accordingly, asset prices tend to gravitate toward the means of normal probability distributions of the present values of their net revenue streams. The present value embodies all the (incomplete) information on the fundamental determinants of net revenue streams while the variance represents errors due to information failures. If the fundamentals remain unchanged, the variance will tend to shrink, but changes in the fundamentals, including unexpected changes in government policies, will increase volatility. Policy intervention will increase efficiency *if and only if* the government has a better understanding of economic efficiency and is better informed than the markets.

While the Fundamental Theorem is about the efficiency of the real economy, the Efficient Markets Hypothesis is about the link between financial markets and those true "fundamentals."[5] Combined they present a picture of economic efficiency being dependent upon free markets for goods, labour and finance, and a minimalist state. Market liberalization is accordingly beneficial because it involves the removal of market distortions, which are *by definition* inefficient.

This approach comes dangerously close to assuming what it purports to prove. Even if the Pareto criterion is accepted as an appropriate definition of efficiency, use of the Fundamental Theorem and the Efficient-Markets Hypothesis presupposes that market conditions correspond, at least approximately, to the conditions necessary for the proof of the Theorem. If they do not, then defining particular market controls as "allocationally inefficient" is a leap of faith.

Five Expected Benefits of Financial Liberalization

A far better approach, and one which corresponds more closely to the realities of economic policy, is to evaluate measures in terms of the attainment of specific goals, such as economic growth, or levels of employment, or the distribution of income, or, at a more microeconomic level, cost minimization, innovation and the growth of markets. In fact, the benefits that are claimed to derive from the liberalization of capital markets are typically presented as a combination of theoretical advantages and practical policy goals. These benefits can be summarized as: [6]

1. In a world of free capital movements, savings will be directed to the most productive investments without regard for national boundaries. Hence, capital will flow from capital-rich developed countries to opportunity-rich emerging economies.
2. Increased competition will create a more efficient financial system, offering better opportunities for savers as well as lower costs for borrowers.
3. New financial instruments such as derivatives (futures, swaps and options), help firms to manage financial risk more effectively.
4. The long-run result should be higher investment and growth.
5. The markets provide a healthy discipline for governments, which encourages better economic policies and performance.[7]

These five claims are predominantly derived from a combination of the conclusions of the Fundamental Theorem:

> Competitive markets will tend to enforce productive efficiency ("savings are directed to the most productive investments") and allocative efficiency ("better opportunities for savers");

together with the Efficient Markets Hypothesis:

> Financial markets operate so as to process information efficiently ("new financial instruments"), and certainly better than governments could ("the markets provide a healthy discipline that encourages better economic policies and performance").

The fundamental difficulty which arises in assessing these claims is, of course, that changes in so many factors other than financial liberalization will have had some impact on the various performance indicators. It is not easy to test the claims for any particular benefit. The proposition that the deregulation of A will lead to higher values of B may appear to be refuted by a fall in B, but it could well be claimed that the fall in B would be even greater if A had not been changed. While statistical tests can never be "conclusive," the only possible response to the problem of counterfactual argument is to assemble as much evidence as possible, identifying as precisely as may be done the role of specific variables and relationships, and, of course, to provide a plausible theory explaining the link between A and B.

COMPARING REALITY WITH EXPECTATIONS

1. Are savings directed towards more productive investments?

If there were truly a single international capital market, then savings would be "directed to the most productive investments without regard for national boundaries." Hence there would be no correlation between the rate of savings in any one nation state and the rate of investment in that nation state. Feldstein and Horioka (1980) assessed the degree of capital market integration by estimating the cross-section equation:

$$(I/Y)_i = \alpha + \beta(S/Y)_i + u_i \tag{1}$$

where I/Y is the ratio of investment to national income, and S/Y the ratio of domestic savings to national income. They found that the estimate of β was close to 1, suggesting a close correlation between investment and national savings, and an absence of international capital market integration. In a recent update of this analysis, Feldstein and Bacchetta (1991) found a value of β equal to 0.79 for the period 1980–1986, still significantly different from zero but lower than the estimate of 0.91 for the 1960s, and 0.86 for the 1970s, a trend confirmed in Feldstein (1994). A very large number of subsequent examinations have found the Feldstein-Horioka result (that β is not significantly different from 1) to be remarkably robust (Coakley, Kulasi and Smith, 1995).

Another way of presenting the same result is to point to the fact that current account imbalances do not, in the medium term, typically amount to large proportions of national income. Even in the 1980s, when current account imbalances rose sharply above earlier ratios (as is consistent with the lower correlation between investment and national savings), they did not exceed 3% of GDP (see Table 2). This compares with the average

UK current account surplus of 4.5% of GDP over the period 1880–1913. Financial liberalization in the modern era may have produced very large *gross* capital flows, but it has not been associated with larger *net* international flows of capital than those experienced under the gold standard before the First World War. One might suspect that the majority of transborder flows may be responding to different incentives from optimizing the allocation of real investment.[8]

Table 2. Current account balance as a proportion of GDP

	1964–1973	1974–1983	1984–1993
Canada	0.85	1.50	2.74
France	0.28	1.06	0.43
Germany	1.11	1.13	2.92
Italy	1.93	1.69	1.08
Japan	1.08	0.78	2.76
United Kingdom	1.33	1.35	1.93
United States	0.40	0.49	2.19

Note: average of *absolute values* of annual ratios of current account balance to GDP.
Source: OECD *National Accounts*, OECD *Main Economic Indicators*.

This *lack* of integration of national capital markets is further indicated by the persistent divergence of real rates of return (Blundell-Wignall and Browne, 1991). Frankel (1992) decomposes the real rate of interest into the covered interest differential, the exchange risk premium and the expected real depreciation. He finds that there has been substantial convergence of covered differentials (as does Marston, 1993) but currency premia (exchange risk plus expected real depreciation) are high. This suggests that differentials in national real rates of return are sustained, at least in part, by the barrier of currency risk. This hypothesis is strengthened by the findings of Sinn (1992) and Bayoumi and Rose (1993) that there is no correlation between regional savings and investment rates *within* countries, and Bayoumi's (1990) finding that there was no correlation between national savings and investment in the gold-standard era. It seems that exchange rate fluctuations inhibit the full integration of capital markets, and provide the opportunity for national governments to pursue relatively independent monetary policies.[9] The existence of separate currencies and national jurisdictions appears to create a more powerful tendency to balance the current account than is the case between regions of a single currency area.[10] The peculiar ability of US to sustain a persistent current account deficit reinforces this conclusion.

That peculiar ability has ensured that the net transfer of resources has not been from the "capital-rich developed countries" to "opportunity-rich emerging economies." The largest net transfer in the period 1983–1992 has been *to* the United States, at an average rate of $100 billion per year. Over the same period, the net transfer to all developing countries amounted to an average of $1 billion per year, and almost all of that inflow was concentrated in the final two years of the period (UN, 1993). Indeed, for most of the 1980s, resources were transferred out of the developing world. During the 1980s, the United States became the world's biggest debtor, hardly an example of capital flowing from capital rich to capital poor. And the flow to the United States has not diminished. In 1994, the net transfer to the United States was $112 billion; in 1995, $119 billion (UN, 1996).

There has, however, been a dramatic change in the mid-1990s with respect to flows to developing countries. In 1993, net transfers to developing countries on an expenditure basis (excluding additions to reserves) rose to $45 billion, in 1994 to $48 billion. Of this latter amount, $20 billion went to Latin America (UN, 1995). These inflows have been the result of capital liberalization, the development of stock markets, and the consequent inflow of portfolio investment, together, in Southeast Asia, with an increase in foreign direct investment. The growth of portfolio investment in Latin America, replacing the bank lending that precipitated the debt crisis, has slackened the credit constraint under which these economies have suffered since the early 1980s. Unfortunately, in Latin America the increase in real investment has been only about one third of the net capital inflow (Devlin, Ffrench-Davis and Griffith-Jones, 1995). The beneficial effects of capital inflows have been overshadowed by the impact of stock market volatility, particularly following the Mexican financial crisis in 1994.

The cautionary comment of Mussa and Goldstein (1993) should be borne in mind: "Over the past two decades, the developing countries that relied most on foreign saving—defined as the top one-third of countries ranked by the ratio of all capital flows to GNP—tended to have higher inflation, higher fiscal deficits, lower investment, and lower growth than those that relied less on foreign saving."

Summing up: while, as noted above, *gross* capital flows have been very large, *net* flows have been very small and have tended to flow toward the developed countries, particularly the United States. Furthermore, flows of finance do not necessarily correspond to flows of real investment. The evidence is not consistent with the claims that the integration of international financial markets has created a market where flows of real savings ignore national boundaries, and in which there has been a flow of capital toward the "opportunity rich" developing world. In so far as there has, in the past five years, been a flow of capital toward "emerging markets," it is a flow that has proved to be very volatile, with investors reluctant to purchase other than the most liquid of financial assets. The role of these emerging markets is discussed further below.

2. Are there better opportunities for savers and lower costs for borrowers?

That liberalization, and the consequent explosion in the size and variety of asset markets, have created a wider range of placement opportunities for savers is undeniable. This is particularly evident in the changing pattern of assets held by institutional investors. In the United States and Japan, the proportion of pension funds' assets invested in foreign securities was negligible in 1980, but by 1993 had risen to over 7% and over 12%, respectively. Over the same period the commitment to foreign assets by British pension funds rose from 10% to over 20% of total assets (Edey and Hviding, 1995, Table 10). The greater choice and spread implicit in portfolio diversification will, *ceteris paribus*, produce welfare gains to savers (Obstfeld, 1993).

The growth of institutional investors (see Table 3) has been a major factor behind the growth of the global capital market. So has financial innovation, which, as noted above, is an essential component of the management of risk. Expanding institutional investment and widening innovation have stimulated each other. The competition between institutional investors manifests itself as a persistent requirement to demonstrate superior returns in order to attract more funds. Successive high short term gains are more effective in this respect than longer term returns. This is so even if over a number of years the overall return on successive short term investments is no greater, and perhaps even somewhat smaller, than a long term investment. An institutional investor pursuing a short term strategy that tops the performance tables in 9 years out of 10, will tend

Table 3. Financial assets managed by collective institutions as a percentage of household financial assets

	1980	1985	1990*
Canada	20.4	24.9	29.7
France	10.6	23.6	36.3
Germany	22.6	29.0	35.1
Italy		2.9	16.1
Japan	15.6	20.2	26.4
United Kingdom	41.5	53.1	58.6
United States	20.0	26.0	31.2

Notes: * for Italy and United Kingdom, 1989. Collective institutions are pension funds and life assurance companies, and collective investment institutions.
Source: BIS (1992).

to attract more funds than the long term investor who performs extremely well once in ten years. Edwards (1993) reports that in the United States "the typical stock is now held for an average of a little over two years, compared to over four years ten years ago and seven years in 1960. The average holding period for institutional investors is less than two years, compared to almost five years for individuals." The enormous flow of funds into institutional hands requires a persistent search for new investment opportunities in which the returns are high and there is a ready opportunity of exit. Innovation is geared towards these two goals.

However, there is no evidence whatsoever that the liberalization of financial markets, and the massive expansion of financial assets that has come in its wake, have led to any lowering of costs to borrowers. On the contrary, in all G7 countries, real interest rates have risen sharply in the 1980s as compared with the Bretton Woods era of capital controls. Other than in the exceptional period of the 1970s, when very high and volatile inflation rates in an era of sharp oil price rises resulted in negative real interest rates in many G7 countries, the period in which capital flows were strictly controlled enjoyed the *lowest* real long term interest rates of modern times. The only comparable period is that from 1933 to 1939, when restrictions were also imposed, and the average real interest rate (for France, Germany, the United Kingdom and the United States) was only 1.7%.

By contrast, real long term interest rates in the 1980s were the *highest* in modern times. This places a very considerable burden on borrowers, whether they are governments or private agents, and greatly increases the danger of national and international debt burdens rising exponentially as real interest rates exceed rates of GDP growth.[11] High interest rates were also typical of the late nineteenth century gold standard, an earlier period of free capital movements, despite the fact that exchange rates were very stable (see Table 4). In neither period of open international financial markets does the prediction of "lower costs for borrowers" correspond to the facts.

These broad observations are reinforced by the findings of Alesina, Grilli and Milesi-Ferretti (1994) and Grilli and Milesi-Ferretti (1995). In analyses that incorporate a range of institutional variables (such as central bank independence and the political leanings of the government), they find that both in a sample of OECD countries, 1950–1989, and in a wider sample of 61 countries, 1966–1989, capital controls are associated with lower real interest rates.

3. Do derivatives help firms to manage financial risk?

The privatization of foreign exchange risk with the collapse of Bretton Woods has been a major motivation behind the liberalization of international capital markets. It is in the foreign exchange markets and the com-

Table 4. Long term real interest rates in the G7

	1870s–1890s	1900–1913	1956–1973	1974–1980	1981–1993
Canada	..	1.6	2.2	0.3	6.7
France	4.2	1.8	1.0	0.4	5.7
Germany	3.4	3.5	3.0	3.0	4.5
Italy	..	..	1.1	−5.0	4.2
Japan	..	..	0.3	0.5	4.4
United Kingdom	2.9	2.7	1.8	−3.3	4.5
United States	6.1	2.3	1.1	−0.3	5.6
Average	4.1	2.6	1.7	0.0	5.1

Notes: Average refers, for all periods, to the average of France, Germany, United Kingdom and the United States. Conversion to real terms is by GDP deflator.
Sources: OECD *Historical Statistics*; OECD *National Accounts*; Homer and Sylla (1991).

modity markets to which they are closely related that derivatives originated, and it is therefore no surprise that increased risk has promoted an enormous expansion in the scale and variety of derivative instruments. The BIS (1996) estimates that the notional principal outstanding in financial derivatives has risen from just over $1,000 billion in 1986, to around $56,500 billion in 1995[12]. A little less than 30% of these are traded instruments, the rest being provided over the counter. Turnover in derivatives markets stood at a daily average of $1,450 billion in 1995, 40% of which comprised exchange traded contracts (BIS, 1996).

The post-Bretton Woods era has been characterized not only by significantly greater fluctuations in exchange rates but also by greater variability in interest rates. Woodall (1995) states that "an estimated 85% of America's *Fortune 500* companies make some use of derivatives to insulate themselves from swings in interest rates and currencies." The growth of derivatives markets is part of the process of liberalization. In a world of fixed rates and capital controls, derivatives had a far smaller role than they do today. It is clearly true that liberalization has spawned derivatives. It is equally true that fluctuating rates and liberalization have *created* the demand for derivatives.[13]

The essence of derivatives trading is the hedging of risk. Risk is, of course, transferred from one side of the transaction to the other. Pooling of risk, by the familiar principle of insurance, simply spreads gains and losses more thinly. Nonetheless, the expansion of derivatives trading has led to some suggestion that risk has actually been increased. In an important sense, this alarm is well-founded. While the underlying risk associated with any given asset may not have changed, the sheer complexity of the structure of derivative positions limits the ability of firms to monitor and manage risk effectively. The well-publicized examples of the abuse of derivatives markets in the cases of Orange County and Barings Bank indicate the difficulties that senior executives may have in understanding what is being done in their names. Similar difficulties are faced by the regulators.[14]

A further element of risk may be introduced by the very mathematical models that are used to price derivatives. Those models are typically derived from the physical sciences and are based on the characteristics of the probability distributions of random movements. The fundamental Black-Scholes model, for example, is based on the assumption that price movements follow the same log-normal distribution as the Brownian motion displayed by many physical phenomena. In fact, as far as price movements are concerned, more price changes tend to be concentrated at the extremes than the log-normal distribution would predict.[15] In these circumstances, the mathematical models that drive much of today's programmed trading will tend to price events at the extremes incorrectly.

Even more important is the problem that may undermine even the best-designed derivatives hedge: liquidity. In 1993, Metallgesellschaft AG, Germany's 14th largest industrial company, was almost ruined by losses in excess of $1 billion suffered in derivatives trading in the oil market by a United States subsidiary and by the refusal of the company's lead banker, Deutsche Bank, to finance the trading strategy further. It is now widely accepted that the hedging strategy employed was misconceived, representing not a hedge but a speculation (Mello and Parsons, 1995). However, Merton Miller and Christopher Culp (1995) have defended Metallgesellschaft's trading strategy, arguing that the fault lay with Deutsche Bank's refusal to fund the financial strategy over the longer period in which it would bear fruit. This raises another issue. Even if it were well-designed, is it right to analyze the hedging strategy *as if* Metallgesellschaft faced a perfect capital market and could therefore borrow virtually unlimited sums today with the prospect of gain a long time in the future? Risk aversion is likely to rise with the scale of indebtedness, a phenomenon that Kalecki (1937) referred to as the "principle of increasing risk."[16] In the Metallgesellschaft case, lack of liquidity created severe problems for the firm alone. Aversion to risk is infectious, rises with indebtedness, and can provoke a general rush to cash that destroys even the most sophisticated hedging strategies and so can pose systemic risk. Liquidity ultimately rests on a diversity of perceptions of asset values. Where there is a tendency for perceptions to be shared and transmitted, there is an enhanced possibility of cumulative liquidity crises. In these circumstances the "management of financial risk" is an illusion.

The proposition that financial liberalization has been accompanied by the benefits of growing numbers of derivatives must therefore be heavily qualified. Liberalization and fluctuating exchange rates have created many of the risks that derivatives are designed to hedge.[17] The growth of derivatives markets may increase systemic risk, both because the very complexity of some derivative instruments and hedging strategies creates severe informational problems for both management and regulators and because derivatives trading may increase exposure to liquidity crises.

4. Has the result been higher investment and growth?

This is the most important test of all, for it derives not from criteria generated within particular theoretical models but from practical policy goals. A higher rate of growth, all other things being equal, results in the higher standards of living that are, after all, the fundamental objective of economic activity. Of course, a simple assertion about the benefits of growth must itself be qualified to take into account any implications for the content and the distribution of national income, and for environmental degradation. But growth and sustainable human development are highly correlated. Hence, for the purpose of this Report, the criterion for distinguishing between beneficial and damaging financial regimes is whether growth is higher or lower, and high rates of investment are presumed to be associated with high growth.[18]

Of course, investment and growth are sensitive to a very wide range of factors. However, disappointing results over the last twenty years throw doubt on the hoped for positive impact of financial liberalization.

Table 5 (which is adapted from Felix, 1995) presents an examination of changes in the share of investment to GDP as between the Bretton Woods era of fixed exchange rates and capital controls (1960–1971) and the current regime of floating rates and open capital markets. The sample of countries covers all OECD, Asian and Latin American countries whose 1983 GDP exceeds $10 billion, all Middle East and North African countries with GDPs above $7.5 billion and all sub-Saharan African countries with GDPs above $5 billion—a total of 54 countries.[19] The comparisons in the table are ordinal because of the variable quality of the data (Felix, 1995, p. 6). In each category, the table presents the number of countries for which the average investment/GDP ratio in that particular decade was higher, or lower, than the 1960–71 average.

It is clear that the predominant tendency has been for investment to fall as a share of GDP. Moreover, declines have become more pronounced in the period 1982–1991 as capital liberalization has become more widespread, with two-thirds of the countries in the sample experiencing declines. Three-quarters of OECD countries had lower investment/GDP ratios in the 1980s than in the 1960s, as did 9 out of 10 Latin American

Table 5. Investment/GDP ratio as compared with the 1960–1971 Average

Number of countries for which the average investment/GDP ratio for the period was higher or lower than the 1960–1971 average.

	1972–1981	1982–1991
All countries (total 54)		
Ratio higher	32	19
Ratio lower	22	35
All non-oil exporting countries (total 45)		
Ratio higher	25	15
Ratio lower	20	30
OECD countries (total 20)		
Ratio higher	7	4
Ratio lower	13	16
Latin America (total 10)		
Ratio higher	7	1
Ratio lower	3	9
East and Southeast Asia (total 7)		
Ratio higher	6	6
Ratio lower	1	1

Notes: *OECD countries are* Australia, Austria, Belgium, Canada, Denmark, Finland, France, Germany, Greece, Ireland, Italy, Japan, Netherlands, New Zealand, Norway, Spain, Sweden, Switzerland, the United Kingdom, the United States. *Latin American countries are* Argentina, Brazil, Chile, Colombia, Dominican Republic, Ecuador, Guatemala, Mexico, Peru and Venezuela. *South and Southeast Asian countries are* Hong Kong, Indonesia, South Korea, Malaysia, Philippines, Singapore and Thailand.
Source: Felix (1995), using as the data source World Bank *World Tables*.

countries. Investment in Latin America had typically been higher in the 1970s but was cut sharply by the accumulation of high levels of indebtedness. Only in East and Southeast Asia was there a persistent pattern of higher rates of investment in the later periods.

Most of the G7 countries also experienced declining investment/GDP ratios in the 1980s, the two exceptions being Canada and Japan.

Given, as was shown above, that investment is highly correlated with domestic savings, a declining ratio of investment to GDP suggests a fall

Table 6. Investment/GDP Ratios in the G7, 1964-1973 and 1983-1992

	A. 1964–1973	B. 1983–1992	B/A
Canada	18.3	21.5	1.17
France	24.0	20.6	0.86
Germany	26.0	20.3	0.78
Italy	26.9	21.3	0.79
Japan	29.7	30.2	1.02
United Kingdom	18.8	17.7	0.94
United States	19.2	18.3	0.95

Note: Gross domestic fixed capital formation as a % of GDP, averaged for each 10-year period.
Source: OECD *National Accounts*, various years

in the overall domestic propensity to save (private plus public). Other things being equal, this will be associated with a lower rate of growth (see Table 7). In developed economies, low levels of investment and slower GDP growth will tend to be accompanied by growing unemployment and declines in *public* saving (often in the form of increasing public deficits), whether due to rising social expenditure or reduced tax revenues. In Japan, where the investment/GDP ratio in the 1980s did not fall,[20] social security spending is particularly low, and high levels of employment have been maintained by the absorption of workers into low-productivity non-financial services (Eatwell, 1995b). In developing countries, a declining share of investment is accompanied by a growing share of output associated with informal employment.

The growth of output per head in the major economies has fallen to between 60% and 30% of the growth rates that prevailed until 1972 (see Table 8). The lesser falls have been experienced in those countries in which growth was relatively low in the earlier period. The inferior economic performance of the G7 countries in the 1980s as compared with the 1960s has also been manifest in rising unemployment and declining rates of productivity growth in the manufacturing industry (Eatwell, 1996).

The overall conclusion is disturbing. Far from there being an increase in investment and growth, the decade of the 1980s (characterized by financial liberalization and very large increases in gross financial flows among countries) has also seen a sharp deterioration in economic performance in the

Table 7. Growth Rate of GDP Per Head, as Compared with the 1960–1971 Average

Number of countries for with the average growth rate for the period was higher or lower than the 1960–1971 average.

	1972–1981	1982–1991
All countries (total 57)		
Growth rate higher	18	10
Growth rate lower	39	47
All non-oil exporting countries (total 48)		
Growth rate higher	11	7
Growth rate lower	37	41
OECD countries (total 20)		
Growth rate higher	1	2
Growth rate lower	19	18
Latin America (total 10)		
Growth rate higher	4	1
Growth rate lower	6	9
East and Southeast Asia (total 7)		
Growth rate higher	5	3
Growth rate lower	2	4

Source: Felix (1995), using as the data source the World Bank *World Tables*.

Table 8. Growth rate of GDP Per Head in the Major Economies

	A. 1961–70	B. 1979–90	B/A
France	5.0	2.0	0.40
Germany	4.3	1.9	0.45
Italy	6.2	1.9	0.31
Japan	9.1	3.0	0.33
United Kingdom	3.3	2.0	0.60
United States	2.3	1.1	0.58

Sources: *European Economy*, Annual Economic Reports; OECD *National Accounts*, 1979–1991.

G7, the OECD as a whole, and in virtually all developing countries with the exception of some countries in East and Southeast Asia. Of course, the fact that liberalization and deteriorating economic performance have coincided does not prove that one has caused the other. But given that inferior economic performance is a common phenomenon, shared by almost all countries, then it is appropriate to look for a common change in circumstances that might have affected them all. The change in the international financial system since 1973 is just such a common change. At any rate, there is no evidence of a link between financial liberalization and higher investment and growth, quite the opposite.[21]

5. Do liberal financial markets provide a healthy discipline which encourages better economic policies?

There can be no doubt at all that liberal financial markets do effect economic policy, sometimes in a quite dramatic manner. Indeed, a common characterization of financial liberalization is that it severely constrains the exercise of discretionary policies by national governments (Bryant, 1987; Keohane and Milner, 1996). But this begs the question of whether the impact is "healthy" and, indeed, how "health" should be defined.

While the first question will be systematically explored in Section 3, the discussion can be introduced here by a few remarks about how "health" should be defined. A minimal definition might be that a healthy economic policy should not contain elements that are in direct contradiction with one another. An excellent example of a policy stance that was internally contradictory was that adopted by the British government in the summer of 1992. At one and the same time, the government attempted, first, to use monetary policy to maintain a fixed parity between the pound and the Dmark, and second, to weather a severe recession characterized by rising unemployment and falling asset values (particularly house prices). However, the level of interest rates required to maintain the external parity exacerbated domestic economic problems. The policy stance became literally incredible. No one could possibly believe that the Government would be prepared to raise interest rates to protect the exchange rate while further depressing domestic asset prices and further deepening the recession. It was this contradiction that was exploited by the financial markets in a speculative run that forced the pound out of the Exchange Rate Mechanism (ERM) and precipitated a 20% devaluation against the Dmark.

While the day of the devaluation has been labelled "Black Wednesday," the event has been hailed by many commentators as a return to rational economic policy and the beginning of the recovery from recession.[22] In this sense the behaviour of the markets may be said to be "healthy" in that they exposed a policy stance that was internally contradictory, but that is all. There is nothing in the markets' behaviour in this case from which to infer any evaluation of the relative merits of using monetary policy *either* to maintain the exchange rate parity *or* to expand the domestic economy. For at the same time as the contradictions of British policy were exposed, the French government managed to convince the markets that it was willing to sacrifice all other policy objectives to the maintenance of the parity between the franc and the Dmark. Once any hint of a contradiction was eliminated, speculation against the French franc ceased.[23]

So a clear distinction must be drawn between the "healthy" exposure of contradictory policies and the "healthy" alignment of policy with a particular theoretical conception of economic efficiency. The former does not depend on any particular theory of the workings of the economy. The latter attempts to identify a desirable or even "ideal" economic policy and relate financial policy to the attainment of that ideal. A desirable policy can be defined only in terms of some expected relationship between action and outcomes, i.e., in terms of a theory of the economy. Neoclassical welfare economics is the dominant theory of economic policy in microeconomics and macroeconomics (although in macroeconomics the prevalence of *ad hoc* theorizing makes for a more varied policy framework). There is even a tendency to identify the conclusions of neoclassical theory with "the fundamentals." Why the relationship between the financial sphere and the real sphere may be less than healthy will be explored in the next section.

Summing up

When confronted with the actual experience of liberalization, the representative list of "benefits" is not convincing. None of the five benefits appear to have been substantially realized, and in many cases the liberalization of international financial markets has been associated with a sharp deterioration in economic performance. Of course, although the accumulation of evidence is disturbing, the coexistence of liberalization and poor economic performance might only be coincidence. Nonetheless, it is worth exploring whether this result can be accounted for by a different analysis of the behaviour of financial markets from that which sustains the conventional wisdom.

3.
Explaining the Record of Liberalization

The issue to be considered is the relationship between the operations of the financial markets and a "healthy" economic policy. The analysis in this section will suggest that the behaviour of financial markets can impose a deflationary bias on the real economy.

FINANCIAL MARKETS AND THE REAL ECONOMY

Two theories of the real economy appear to play a major role in forming the perceptions of financial market operators. The first deals with unemployment, the second with fiscal deficits.

The Non-Inflation Accelerating Rate of Unemployment

The behaviour of the bond markets today suggests a prevailing market view according to which, other than in the most depressed conditions, any indication of higher levels of activity and employment will result in higher interest rates. The fear of impending increases in interest rates and of consequent capital losses precipitates a sell-off in the bond market, raising the long term rate of interest, as expected. Depending upon the national origins of the sell-off, the exchange rate may rise as well. Higher interest rates, whether or not aided and abetted by a higher exchange rate, tend to result in a slowdown in the growth in output and employment, aborting policies designed to increase activity.

The presumed link between activity and accelerating inflation is associated with the concept of a natural rate of unemployment (Friedman, 1968; Phelps, 1968). If, as the natural rate hypothesis suggests, the economy has a persistent tendency to gravitate towards the natural rate, deviating from it only in the short run, then any systematic upswing in activity will precipitate accelerating inflation with upward pressure on interest rates.[24] But is the hypothesis correct? Does it indeed truly represent the "fundamentals" of the real economy? If not, then the actions of the financial markets are not "healthy."

Some doubt is cast on the value of the concept of the natural rate by its propensity to shadow the actual rate of unemployment. In 1970, with actual unemployment at 4.8%, the *Economic Report of the President* suggested that the natural rate of unemployment in the United States was 3.8%. In 1979, with the actual rate at 5.8%, the estimated natural rate had risen to 5.1%. By 1983, with the actual rate at 9%, the *Economic Report of the President* estimated the natural rate at 7% (Gordon, 1987). Commenting on a similar peripatetic tendency of the "natural rate" in European economies, Robert Solow (1990) argues that "European experience can only be taken as evidence against the meaningfulness of a stable and well-defined natural rate . . . Attempts to salvage the idea of a well-defined equilibrium unemployment rate require the equilibrium rate itself to have undergone drastic change between the 1970s and the 1980s. To any reasonably sceptical person, it all smacks of the invocation of epicycles to salvage Ptolemaic astronomy, but apparently with rather less success."[25]

Solow points to evidence that the relationship between inflation and unemployment can be altered by macroeconomic policy. Just as the low growth of the past decade has raised the natural rate, so boosting demand, while it may raise inflation in the short run, will in due course lower the natural rate. In other words, active macroeconomic policy could be a way to cure "structural" unemployment. Yet, it is exactly the possibility of a short term increase in inflation that alarms the bond market, and results in the negation of expansionary policies. The bond market behaves as if the economy is at or about the natural rate of unemployment. The higher levels of unemployment characteristic of the 1980s may be in part attributable to this persistent tendency of the bond market to regard the current rate of unemployment as the natural rate. Reaction to changes in the level of activity are typically asymmetric: all increases in activity are likely to precipitate falling bond prices while decreases in activity are evidence of praise-worthy financial discipline.

Markets' Reactions to Fiscal Deficits

The impact of the natural-rate hypothesis on market behaviour is reinforced by the markets' attitude to fiscal deficits. Increases in fiscal deficits are believed to be inflationary and to precipitate increases in interest rates. Consequently, deficits incur the displeasure of the bond market. There is a clear relationship between national budget deficits and the real rate of interest (Orr, Edey and Kennedy, 1995; BIS, 1995). Once again the market is imposing persistent deflationary pressure.

Other than in exceptional years, the current account balances of the OECD countries taken as a whole fluctuate closely around zero. Accordingly, the sum of fiscal deficits must be equal to the excess of private savings over private investment, i.e., roughly

$$\Sigma_i(G - T) = \Sigma_i(S - I) \qquad (2)$$

where G is government expenditure, T is tax revenue, S is private-sector saving, I is private-sector investment, and Σ_i indicates the summation over all OECD countries.

The decline in investment and in activity that has been characteristic of the 1980s will tend inevitably to be associated with rising fiscal deficits. The problem is: which causes which? Similarly, the steady increase in public sector debt that has been another characteristic of the 1980s may be not so much a product of profligate government borrowing in liberalized capital markets as a result of the decline in investment relative to private sector saving.[26] In both cases, the theoretical issue is whether the causal relationships between the financial balance of the government sector and the financial balance of the private sector can be clearly identified. Which are the independent variables and which the dependent variables?

The theory underpinning the bond market response to public-sector deficits is the fiscal counterpart to the natural-rate hypothesis. Just as the operation of the competitive labour market is supposed to ensure that the economy always gravitates towards the natural rate of unemployment, so the operation of a competitive capital market is supposed to ensure the balance between savings and investment at the natural rate. Accordingly, it is argued that government deficits "crowd out" private-sector investment and, indeed, as equation (2) indicates, public deficits must be accompanied by an excess of private savings over private investment. The increase in private savings is, according to the Ricardian Equivalence Theorem, a rational consumer reaction to the increase in government debt (Barro, 1974). However, investigation of the "crowding-out" phenomenon has indicated that crowding-out is a characteristic of the operations of financial markets, not of the underlying real economy (Blanchard, 1987). This in turn suggests that the behaviour of the financial markets is creating a self-fulfilling prophecy: public spending crowds out private investment because the market reaction to public spending is to raise long term interest rates. The high interest rates demanded by the bond markets tend to produce downward pressures on private-sector investment and upward pressures on the private savings rate, further exacerbating fiscal deficits.

The typical reaction of bond markets to changes in the labour market and in the government's fiscal stance suggests that they behave as if the economy will tend to be in a perfectly competitive equilibrium, ensuring that there is an underlying tendency towards full employment and an efficient allocation of resources. If this is not a true model of the economy, i.e., if the economy does not operate in this fashion, then the markets' "discipline" may well be inappropriate and damaging. This will be particularly true if the financial markets operate in a manner that is in some respects self-fulfilling, i.e., the market determines the fundamentals—which leads us to a quite different explanation of the relationship between financial markets and the real economy.

HOW MARKET VIEWS ARE FORMED

The interpretation of the impact of financial market liberalization is, as has been seen above, heavily dependent upon the theory of the real economy and of the interaction between the real economy and financial markets. An examination of how market views are formed suggests an alternative to the orthodox combination of neoclassical welfare economics and the efficient markets hypothesis. In this alternative theory, the level of output in the economy is determined by the level of effective demand,

and it is assumed that there is no tendency for that demand to gravitate to a level commensurate with full employment growth. Financial markets influence output, and the trend of output, via their impact on effective demand.[27]

In his *General Theory*, Keynes provided quite a different description of financial market behaviour, and of the interaction between real and financial markets, from that assumed by the conventional wisdom. Keynes likened the operations of financial markets to a "beauty contest." He was not referring to a 1930s equivalent of the Miss World contest, in which judges declare a winner. He had in mind a competition then popular in the British tabloid Sunday press in which readers were asked to rank pictures of young women in the order that they believed would correspond to the average preferences of the competitors as a whole. So in order to win, the player should not express his or her own preferences, nor even the genuine preferences of average opinion, but instead should anticipate "what average opinion expects average opinion to be" (Keynes, 1936, p. 156). In the same way, the key to success in the financial markets is not what the individual investor considers to be the virtues or otherwise of any particular policy but what he or she believes everyone else in the market will believe everyone else will think.

Since the markets are driven by average opinion about what average opinion will be, an enormous premium is placed on any information or signals that might provide a guide to the swings in average opinion and to how average opinion will react to changing events. These signals must be simple and clear-cut. Sophisticated interpretations of the economic data would not provide a clear lead. Hence the money markets and foreign exchange markets become dominated by simple slogans—larger fiscal deficits lead to higher interest rates, an increased money supply results in higher inflation, public expenditure is bad, falling unemployment always leads to accelerating inflation, and so on.

However, such slogans could not dominate market behaviour if the simple economic propositions embedded within them were consistently shown to be false. Profits could be earned by those who ignore the slogans, those, for example, who buy bonds as unemployment falls or fiscal deficits rise. If such behaviour were to be successful, "average opinion" would tend to change. So if the "true model" of the real economy were the neoclassical model, then "average opinion" would tend to oscillate around the predictions of neoclassical theory. The peculiarity of the Keynesian model is that monetary and financial factors are assigned a dominant role in the determination of real economic performance. The "true model" is not independent of the behaviour of financial markets. It is therefore possible for "average opinion" to become self-fulfilling. If the markets believe that higher fiscal deficits result in higher real rates of interest, then so they will. Of course, "average opinion" is not formed in a vacuum. It has its own history and is heavily influenced by fashionable theories and by the exercise of the financial powers of national governments, particularly the more economically powerful ones. The recent history of capital market liberalization might be represented as a swing in the balance of influence from a post-war theory of economic policy that enjoined national governments to limit international capital movements, to the present-day theory that encourages free capital movements and the abdication of national regulatory powers.[28]

Keynes's characterization of the operation of financial markets suggests two ways in which financial market liberalization might result in a deterioration in overall economic performance. First, a market that operates as a beauty contest is likely to be highly unstable and prone to occasional severe loss of liquidity as all opinion tends to shift in the same direction. This will increase the cost of capital and sometimes lead to severe capital shortages—both factors that will tend to discourage investment and reduce levels of activity in the medium term. Second, the operation of the beauty contest in a liberal environment may produce systematic changes in the behaviour of both public and private sectors. Although these changes may succeed in reducing instability, they achieve this only at the cost of a medium-term deterioration in overall economic performance. Both effects, which have bearings on policy-making, will be introduced here.

CONSEQUENCES FOR PUBLIC POLICY

An Erratic Discipline

The tendency of financial markets to move erratically is an important qualification of the alleged "healthy" discipline they impose on governments. Woodall (1995) quotes the IMF as arguing that "the discipline exercised by capital markets over policy is neither infallible nor is it applied smoothly and consistently" and herself suggests that "discipline is often doled out erratically, with waves of excessive optimism being followed by excessive pessimism." There have been three recent prominent examples of erratic market behaviour: first, the rise and fall of the dollar in the 1980s—the index of the dollar effective exchange rate swung from 105 in 1980 to 145 in 1985 to 100 in 1990;[29] second, the rise and fall of world bond markets in 1993 and 1994; and third, the crisis of the Mexican peso at the end of 1994. What is particularly striking about the second and third examples is that they are both clearly linked to financial market liberalization.[30]

As far as the fluctuations in the bond market are concerned, the BIS (1995) attributes the fall of bond prices to:

(a) Overshooting in 1993 (i.e., excessively high prices).
(b) Speculative excesses fuelled by "leverage which allowed participants to take large exposures with relatively little own capital, either by borrowing or using derivatives."
(c) "Institutional features and market practices" including hedging strategies.

Moreover, "an important force linking yield movements across markets was the generalised retrenchment by non-resident, especially US, investors."

The overall conclusion is that there is significant potential for "medium-term deviations from realistic views about sustainable levels (fundamentals) . . . Such misalignments have great potential costs in terms of a misallocation of resources. They also heighten the risk of abrupt and disorderly corrections and hence of broader financial instability" (BIS, 1995, p. 116).

It was just such a "disorderly correction" that in 1995 forced the United States and the IMF into the unaccustomed role of lender of last resort to the Mexican money markets and compelled Mexico to increase its already crippling burden of foreign debt. Mexico had been pursuing the policy stance recommended by the IMF: a stable exchange rate with the dollar to act as a "nominal peg" to the inflation rate, and liberalization of capital markets (by selling dollar-denominated instruments). As the stable exchange rate encouraged imports, capital flowed in to cover the deficit and acquire a 20% return. The possibility of devaluation, a perfectly rational step in the light of Mexico's steadily deteriorating current account and overly restrictive monetary policy, produced a dramatic rush out of Mexican paper, provoking a classic liquidity crisis and real recession in Mexico (Taylor and Schlefer, 1995). As the BIS (1995) comments, the crisis was precipitated by financial factors despite the fact that "external deficits in Mexico have this time coincided with both microeconomic and macroeconomic 'fundamentals' that were healthy by any standards." The Mexican economy, far from staying "healthy," became distinctly "unhealthy," with severe social consequences.

The Mexican example also exposes an ambiguity in the use of the term "fundamentals." In some discussions, this term is used to suggest the "true model" of the economy. In others, it is used more pragmatically to mean simply a position that is sustainable. Of course, if the "true model" is indeed "true," then these two interpretations can amount to the same thing. But if it is not, then the definition of what is sustainable may itself be a function of self-fulfilling behaviour of the financial markets.

If financial markets are to promote "healthy" policy, then the model of the economy implicit in market behaviour must be a "true" model, for if it is not, the discipline enforced by markets may not be healthy. This does not mean that the outcome implied by market behaviour will not indeed be forthcoming, only that that outcome will not necessarily correspond to real economic efficiency. There is nothing efficient about zero inflation and 10% unemployment, for example. If market behaviour is not based on a true model, or if the performance of the real economy is not independent of financial market behaviour, then erratic and disorderly market movements are not merely "overshooting" or temporary fluctuations around a true mean. They may be the determinants of systematically inefficient behaviour.

Governments in Search of Credibility

The liberalization of financial markets has clearly reduced the power of governments to manipulate the economy. In fixed exchange rate systems (such as the ERM), governments face the "impossibility problem": the impossibility of sustaining fixed exchange rates, free capital movements and an independent monetary policy. With flexible exchange rates, control over short term rates is recovered, to some degree, but long term rates are still subject to the whims and judgements of the international bond traders. Moreover, control over short term rates is only recovered if, like the United States Federal Reserve Bank, the authorities are apparently unconcerned about movements in the exchange rate,[31]—a rare luxury, and perhaps a costly one. The markets also place powerful constraints on the exercise of fiscal policy. Orr, Edey and Kennedy (1995) find that real interest rates are highest in countries with the largest structural budget deficits and current account deficits (other than the United States).

If the financial markets are simply enforcing the logic of real economic efficiency, strengthening the self-adjusting powers of competitive markets, then the "disciplining" of governments would be benign, but if markets are pursuing the rules of a beauty contest and imposing self-fulfilling prejudices on the workings of the real economy, then the outcome may be very damaging. The overwhelming scale of potential capital flows means that governments must today, as never before, attempt to maintain market "credibility." Credibility has become the key-stone of policy making in the nineties (King, 1995). A credible government is a government which pursues a policy that is "market friendly" that is, a policy that is in accordance with what the markets believe to be "sound" and "efficient." Particularly favoured are measures designed to meet a "prudent" pre-determined monetary target or imposing nominal anchors on monetary policy, and balancing the budget (preferably by cutting public expenditure rather than raising taxes). Governments that fail to pursue "sound" and "prudent" policies are forced to pay a premium on the interest costs of financing their programmes. Severe loss of credibility will lead to a financial crisis. The determination of what is credible, and how governments lose credibility, is a product of the beauty contest.

The BIS (1995) sums up the situation:

> "In the financial landscape which has been emerging over the past two decades, the likelihood of extreme price movements may well be greater and their consequences in all probability further reaching.... At the macro level, the new landscape puts a premium on policies conducive to financial discipline. Strategically, a firm longer-term focus on price stability is the best safeguard, one which can only be achieved with the support of fiscal discipline."

The BIS then warns, "yet such a safeguard is by no means always effective."

The costs of losing credibility can reverberate over many years and reacquiring credibility can be very costly in real terms. So if governments are risk-averse, the demands of credibility will impose broadly deflationary macroeconomic strategies. In the 1960s, the managed international financial framework permitted expansionary, full employment policies which were contagious both domestically, encouraging private investment, and internationally, underwriting the growth of world trade. In the 1980s, the deregulated financial framework has encouraged policies that elevate financial stability above growth and employment. This has ratchetted up real interest rates, which have in turn reduced domestic investment, reduced the growth of world trade and slowed the rate of growth of effective demand.

All this is not surprising in the light of the basic Keynesian proposition that the real economy is not self-adjusting, i.e., that markets are just as likely to settle in a low-growth, high unemployment equilibrium as in any other. Keynes pointed out that the idea of self-adjustment was convincing only because of a common confusion between the efficiency that the market may impose on the operations of an individual firm and the fact that the market does not ensure that the economy as a whole is maintaining an efficient level of employment, or, in a longer-term perspective, an efficient balance between consumption and investment. In Keynes's characterization of the operations of a market economy, it is clear that the behaviour of financial markets may well be an important factor driving the economy towards a low-growth, high-unemployment equilibrium. The markets are neither omniscient nor benign. When their influence is combined with the persistent search for government "credibility," defined in terms of "sound money" and "prudent" deflationary policies, then the low level position is the most likely outcome.

4.
Liberal Financial Markets and the Private Sector

It has been argued above that liberalized financial markets have imposed deflationary pressures on world levels of growth, productivity and investment. These pressures on both public and private sectors derive primarily from the sheer scale of potential capital flows, and from the potential volatility of those flows.

Volatile financial markets generate economic inefficiencies. Even if fluctuations take place around a "true" level, volatility creates financial risk. Even if the facilities exist for hedging that risk, the cost of financial commitment is raised. More generally, volatility may well result in decisions being made on the basis of false information, and may induce a general reluctance to take any step that will increase exposure to unpredictable fluctuations in exchange rates or interest rates. A simple premise might be: the greater the volatility, the greater the reluctance to undertake any exposure to fluctuating variables. The greatest danger of all in open capital markets is, of course, posed by a general loss of liquidity.

A further question raised by the liberalization of international capital markets is the extent to which instability is transmitted between markets. As has often been noted, one of the most interesting aspects of the stock market crash in October 1987 is that it was a world-wide phenomenon. Prices were marked down in all stock markets around the world with no particular reference to the "fundamentals" in each particular country. It is now generally accepted that this was a classic example of "contagion," of a beauty contest in which markets were reacting to the news of markets. King and Wadhwani (1988) have shown "that the correlation coefficient between hourly changes in London and New York rose after the crash, an observation that is consistent with the idea that the extent of contagion grew after October 19th. When we allow for time zone trading and examine interactions between Tokyo, London and New York in turn, this finding is confirmed. . . . the value of the contagion coefficient measuring the impact of New York on London depends on volatility."

DEVELOPED ECONOMIES

Analyses of financial instability typically focus on short term volatility, often monthly or even daily price movements. It is not surprising to find that short term volatility in money markets has increased since the end of the Bretton Woods system. On average, the monthly volatility of G7 exchange rates has tripled, with far larger increases in volatility being experienced by countries outside the core of the ERM. There has been no tendency for volatility to decrease in the 1980s and early 1990s, but equally, after the sharp increase between the 1960s and early 1980s, there has been no further tendency for volatility to increase despite the fact that currency trading has increased enormously (see Table 9). There is a clear link between international speculative flows, the exit of Italy and the United

Table 9. Volatility of Effective Exchange Rates

	1960–1969	1980–1985	1986–1989	1990–1994
Canada	0.2	0.9	1.0	1.1
France	1.0	1.1	0.8	0.7
Germany	0.7	1.0	0.8	0.9
Italy	0.3	0.7	0.6	1.9
Japan	0.3	2.4	2.4	2.4
United Kingdom	1.0	2.0	1.8	2.0
United States	0.2	1.8	2.1	1.5

Note: standard deviation of monthly changes (percentage points)
Source: Edey and Hviding (1995).

Kingdom from the ERM in 1992, and the greater exchange rate volatility subsequently experienced by those countries.

As shown in Table 10, similar increase in volatility is evident in bond yields although this, too, has generally eased a little in the 1990s *when international bond trading has increased sharply*. There has also been some correspondence between short and long rates, with increased volatility of short term interest rates, too (Shiller, 1988).

No consistent trend toward increased volatility is observable in equity markets either, even though volatility was a little higher in the 1980s—see Table 11. Stock market volatility has been shown to be only weakly related to volatility in the real economy, although William Schwert (1989)

Table 10. Volatility of Bond Yields

	1960–1969	1980–1985	1986–1989	1990–1994
Canada	0.13	0.58	0.27	0.31
France	0.11	0.42	0.38	0.31
Germany	0.10	0.28	0.20	0.22
Italy	0.11	0.43	0.37	0.46
Japan	0.27	0.37	0.52	0.38
United Kingdom	0.17	0.43	0.43	0.36
United States	0.18	0.58	0.34	0.23

Note: standard deviation of monthly changes (percentage points)
Source: Edey and Hviding (1995).

Table 11. Volatility of Share Prices

	1960–1969	1980–1985	1986–1989	1990–1994
Canada	3.5	5.7	5.0	3.5
France	4.6	7.2	7.9	5.3
Germany	4.0	3.0	6.1	4.1
Italy	5.0	6.5	7.8	6.6
Japan	4.3	2.6	4.1	5.8
United Kingdom	3.5	3.4	5.7	3.7
United States	6.9	3.8	3.9	2.8

Note: standard deviation of monthly changes (percentage points)
Source: Edey and Hviding (1995).

has argued that there is a link, albeit a weak link, between volatility and recession.

There is only limited evidence of a significant impact of short term financial volatility on the real economy. Writing in the early 1980s, Andrew Crockett (1984), argued that "The large majority of empirical studies on the impact of exchange rate variability on the volume of international trade are unable to establish a systematically significant link between measured exchange rate variability and the volume of international trade." Joseph Gagnon (1993), in an analytical study, suggested that the impact of volatility on trade is likely to be negative but small. Examining the wider impact on the real economy with data covering 49 countries, Baxter and Stockman (1989) found no link between the performance of the real economy and the exchange rate regime (fixed or floating). However, an empirical study by Linda Goldberg (1993) found that exchange rate volatility had a clear negative impact on investment in United States industry, although the observed negative effects were quantitatively small. Her results are in accord with John Huizinga's findings (1994) that "for United States manufacturing industries the move to flexible exchange rates was in fact accompanied by significant and widespread increases in uncertainty about real wages, the real price of materials inputs, the real output price . . . . Higher uncertainty about real output price was shown to be negatively correlated with the investment rate and productivity growth . . . Higher uncertainty about real wages was also . . . negatively correlated with the investment rate, but positively correlated with productivity growth. Higher uncertainty about the real price of materials inputs was . . . positively correlated with the investment rate and productivity growth."

Huizinga's study distinguishes between periods of fixed and fluctuating rates, rather than using measures of volatility as such. In doing so he illuminated an important point. It would appear that short term volatility in exchange rates is not the relevant measure for the impact of international capital liberalization on the medium-term performance of the real economy. Liberalization was accompanied in the 1970s and 1980s by huge medium-term swings in exchange rates, with no obvious relationship to the needs of the real economy. For example, the appreciation of the sterling effective exchange rate by over 20% between 1978 and 1981 was accompanied by a doubling of the inflation rate in the United Kingdom. The consequent increase in the real exchange rate resulted in a rapid deterioration in the balance of trade in manufactured goods and a fall in domestic manufacturing output of 20%, declines from which British manufacturing has not fully recovered. Similarly the 40% swings in the US effective exchange rate in the 1980s were associated with the growth of the US current account deficit to over $160 billion in 1987 (with a counterpart deterioration in the Federal budget deficit).

Giorgia Giovanetti (1991) has shown that the impact on competitiveness of a given change in a fluctuating rate is significantly less than the same change in a fixed, but adjustable, exchange rate. The rationale of this result is not hard to find. Under a fixed rate system, an adjustment of the rate results in a new pattern of international prices that can be used, with reasonable confidence, as a framework for long term decision making. The same absolute change in a fluctuating exchange rate will not be expected to persist in the same way, and therefore will be less of an incentive for long term change. Of course, exchange rate movements today are far more effected by changes in asset prices than by the requirements of purchasing power parity. But in so far as altering exchange rates is a means of adjusting to differences in international competitiveness, then fluctuating rates, by the very nature of the uncertainties that they create, will require larger swings in relative parities than are really appropriate—a further contribution to international instability.

As well as exchange rate instability, the 1980s have also experienced both an increase in the volatility of bond rates and a sharp increase in the real level of the long term bond rate. There is a clear body of evidence that links the volatility and high rates of return demanded in deregulated capital markets to bond default and corporate failure. Gertler and Hubbard (1988) have argued that the impact of volatility on a firm's net worth will limit its ability to borrow, and that smaller firms can be hard hit by the impact of high interest rates on the cost of loans. Combined with the well-known evidence presented by Fazzari, Hubbard and Petersen (1988) that retained profits are the key determinant of investment, these results suggest that the impact of high and volatile interest rates on cash flow will lead to a significant deterioration in corporate performance, especially for those companies with high debt-equity ratios.

In a short briefing paper, Keating and Wilmot (1992) present a startling illustration of the impact of the creation and demise of the Bretton Woods system on the default rate on corporate bonds (see Figure 1). The Bretton

Figure 1: Default Rate in US Corporate Bonds, 1900–91

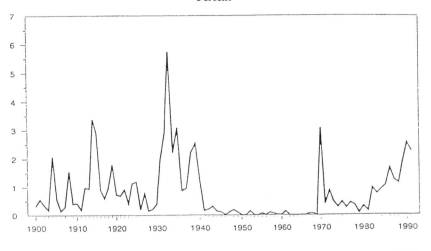

Source: Keating and Wilmot (1992)

Woods era is characterized by historically low default rates, while default rose rise sharply as that era ended, and have climbed steadily through the 1980s. This pattern of the impact of liberalization on corporate survival is confirmed by a study of United States business failures by Michele Naples and Arben Arifaj (1995). Naples and Arifaj verify the fact that the corporate failure rate was peculiarly low in the Bretton Woods era and rose sharply in the 1980s. They also find that the real interest rate and the corporate debt-equity ratio are significant explanatory variables of that failure rate.

What is particularly striking about these observations is that they suggest that deregulation of national and international capital markets has raised the cost of capital and introduced instability into the local financial environment of middle America. The corporate survival rate was sustained in the Bretton Woods era by a combination of macroeconomic steady growth and the micro-economic benefits of low interest rates and financial stability. Globalization of financial markets has meant that, whereas international disequilibria may, in the past, have been manifest in exchange rate movements, today they have an impact on interest rates in domestic money markets. The instability of local interest rates means that international financial pressures are felt by small and medium-sized firms operating in local markets, and not only by large companies operating internationally.

EMERGING MARKETS

As was noted above, the growth of equity markets in developing countries has played a positive role in encouraging a flow of capital towards developing countries and relaxing financial constraints on economic activity, particularly in Latin America (Devlin, Ffrench-Davis and Griffith-Jones, 1995). The World Bank, through the International Finance Corporation, is actively encouraging the development of equity markets in developing countries and encouraging them to liberalize their capital markets as the most effective way of attracting international capital. The conventional wisdom is effectively summed up in a report by the World Institute of Development Economics Research (1990), that called for the repeal of Article VI of the IMF Articles of Agreement:

> "The need to attract foreign capital in non-debt creating forms *is only one reason, and not the most important reason, why developing countries should wish to foster their emerging equity markets.* Equity markets are a vital part of economic development -they encourage savings, help channel savings into productive investment and encourage entrepreneurs to improve the efficiency of investments. This Report therefore puts the role of the foreign investor within the context of the general desirability of the growth of equity markets for domestic resource mobilisation reasons as well as for tapping foreign savings and know-how on market organization and technology."

As Singh (1993) points out, this argument fails to take account of the substantial body of literature that demonstrates that relatively sophisticated equity markets in developed countries are not effective either in ensuring an efficient allocation of savings or in encouraging efficient decision making by entrepreneurs. It also ignores the widely accepted view that "bank-based" systems of corporate finance have superior development records than do "stock-market based" systems (Frank and Mayer, 1990; Pollin, 1995). Moreover, Singh reports that "there is little or no evidence of an increase in aggregate savings for most developing countries as a result of greater new issues activity on the stock market. In some of the countries (e.g. Mexico, Turkey) aggregate savings actually fell during the 1980s" (Singh, 1993).[32]

However, Singh and Hamid (1991) have shown that even though the development of stock markets does not increase savings, equity finance is nonetheless a very important *form* of funding for industry.[33] New issues are far more important in the funding of manufacturing companies in developing countries than is the case in developed countries, where new equity finance is a very small component of the corporate flow of funds. Whereas in United States industrial companies, retained earnings provide over 90% of the corporate sources of funds (Corbett and Jenkinson, 1994), in South Korea only 13% of funds were internally generated and across the entire sample, an average of 32% of funds were internally generated. Although there were very wide differences between countries, new equity provided, on average, 40% of funds in the developing economies compared with a *negative* contribution (due to takeover activity and "buy backs") of 9% in the United States.

Given the importance of new issues in the financing of corporate growth in developing countries a cloud is cast over the success of emerging markets in attracting capital flows to developing countries by the very high volatility of those markets. The short term volatility of stock prices is significantly greater than in the G-7. Over the period 1985–1989, the standard deviation of monthly price changes was 37 in Argentina, 21 in Brazil, 8 in South Korea, 15 in Taiwan, and 24 in Turkey (compare the figures for developed countries in Table 11).

Of even greater importance are the violent medium-term swings to which these markets are prone. Singh (1993) reports that "between 1982 and 1985, share prices of the Brazilian stock exchange rose five fold (in US dollar terms), two years later they had fallen to 28% of their 1985 value. In the first nine months of 1987, share prices on the Mexican market rose 6-fold. However, in October 1987 prices fell to a tenth of their previous level. In Taiwan, the largest Third World stock market, between 1987 and February 1990 the share price index rose by 330 percent to reach a peak of 12,600, the index then fell to a quarter of its value (3160) by

September 1990." It is difficult to associate such volatility with efficiency or to consider it mere "overshooting."[34] Instability is also likely to discourage international capital flows into emerging markets and provoke the sort of liquidity crisis suffered in Mexico. The BIS (1995) comments that "capital inflows—inflated by volatile short term movements—can reach levels that are not sustainable. In the process, the exchange rate and other financial asset prices can overreact in ways that are inimical to long term goals. . . . In some countries, recent developments in securities markets have constituted a potential source of systemic risk." In the light of recent experience, both the BIS and the IMF have recommended that developing countries consider imposing short term capital controls to discourage excessive capital inflow.

5.
Conclusions

Effects of Liberalized Financial Markets

The broad lines of a potential explanation of the relationship between liberalized international financial markets and the performance of the real economy can now be discerned. Given that financial markets operate as a beauty contest and the real economy has no automatic tendency to converge to full-employment growth, then the simple rules of the game embodied in the policy positions believed by market participants to be held by other participants will be imposed on the economy. The downside risks involved in flaunting the rules of the game will create a deflationary bias in government policy and in the private sector of the real economy. This is reinforced by the very high costs of debt in a situation in which real interest rates typically exceed growth rates by a substantial margin. High interest rates are themselves the outcome of the attempt to maintain financial stability in a potentially volatile world. So the post-war goal of "a high and stable level of employment" is abandoned and replaced by the goals of "long term price stability"—the path to which is defined according to the rules of the game.

The easing of bond yield volatility in the 1990's probably reflects widespread adjustments to financial market constraints, rather than improvements in the functioning of the markets themselves. Policy has been adjusted to accommodate the pressures of volatile markets, and this explains the decline in the instability observed in recent years. Private sector decision makers have also adapted to the new low-level situation. With governments no longer committed to the maintenance of full employment levels of effective demand, the prospective growth of sales is reduced and the attractions of investment curtailed. Falling private sector investment will tend to precipitate some deterioration in the government's fiscal balance, further exacerbating deflationary pressures.

It is *potential* volatility that creates the pressures on government policy. As governments increasingly accept the new rules, and as demands for "international surveillance" and "openness" enforce those rules with increasing ferocity, observed volatility may diminish.[35] A relatively slow growth, high unemployment, monetarily stable system can endure indefinitely. This is the case even in circumstances of rapid technological change. New technologies might be expected to spark off a Schumpeterian wave of new investment, but with macroeconomic balances maintained in a carefully constructed deflationary stance, the impact of new technologies is felt more on the composition of activity than on the rate of growth. The low overall rate of growth ensures that the average rate of productivity growth remains low (Eatwell, 1995b).

A low rate of growth, with low ratios of investment and saving to GDP will not lessen the influence of the bond market. Even though the flow of savings may be diminished, the stock of financial assets remains enormous and it is the turnover of that stock which determines long term interest rates. As liquidity increases with the creation of ever more sophisticated financial products, the stock market begins to operate like a bond market. Institutional investors increasingly demand that dividend rates should be maintained, irrespective of corporate performance, thereby imposing a further deflationary burden on corporate cash flow.

In sum, a liberalized, sophisticated financial system, with a premium placed on the possibility of exit, is a fragile financial system. That fragility is manifest:

(a) in liquidity crises, some of which have substantial reverberations in reduced real output;

(b) in risk aversion in the private sector, which produces a bias towards the short term and a corresponding reluctance to invest for the long term;
(c) in risk aversion in the public sector, producing a bias towards deflationary policies; and
(d) in persistent demands for greater "flexibility" to increase the possibilities of exit.

The development of new derivative products to manage the risk that the liberal financial system has itself created has in turn produced new systemic risks. Indeed, the complexity of such instruments leaves them vulnerable to sudden loss of liquidity as opinion swings in one direction or another.

The explanation presented here of the impact of international capital liberalization is consistent with the deterioration of economic performance in the post-Bretton Woods era. It does not, of course, *prove* causation. It simply comprises a set of hypotheses on the operation of financial markets and the real economy, and the interaction between them, which would suggest that liberal financial markets with very high turnover would tend to impose deflationary pressures on the economy.[36] As regards developing economies, the benefits that the abolition of financial controls have brought to emerging markets must be heavily qualified by the instability that is inherent in the ease of exit demanded by investors. Granted, increased flows of direct, real investment probably require agreement to unrestricted repatriation of profits—but probably not the instant exit conditions demanded by financial markets.

Lessons Learnt

If the foregoing hypotheses do indeed capture the essence of the current operation of the international economy, this raises the question of what could be done to improve the relationship between the operation of the international financial system and the overall efficiency of the real economies of the world. It is often argued that nothing can be done to change the present system since capital flows can overwhelm a large number of measures decided by any one government. This is certainly true. But it is equally true that the foundation stones of the world financial system are the monetary instruments issued by a small number of major governments. The US dollar, the Dmark, the yen, and the pound sterling were on at least one side of the transaction in 80% of currency trades in 1989 and 1992, and 77% of trades in 1995 (BIS, 1996, table F-3). Ultimately, those governments acting together have the potential to control capital flows.[37]

But that potential will only be manifest if governments themselves espouse a different theory of economic policy than the orthodox view that currently dominates economic and political debate. In many cases the assumed superiority of a liberal market strategy derives not just from conventional theory but also from a belief in the inherent economic incompetence and even venality of governments—an unflattering picture that some governments themselves seem to have adopted. Of course, there are a number of examples for which such pessimism is justified. Yet in the longer term successful economic development has always been associated with active developmental states (Gerschenkron, 1962; Amsden, 1989; Singh, 1994). State intervention has also contributed to short-run efficiency. Within the Bretton Woods system, active macroeconomic management was successful in maintaining high levels of output and employment (Eichengreen, 1993). Examples of bad and incompetent policy are not sufficient justification for handing the future of the economy over to an economic environment of liberalized markets that renders systematic policy-making impossible. Rather, they should encourage the creation of an environment within which good and competent policy can be effective.

As was argued above, restrictions of capital flows have not necessarily been associated with poor economic performance. It is worth remembering that western reconstruction after World War II, surely one of the great economic policy achievements of modern times, was conducted in an environment of tight capital controls. Even current account convertibility was typically not permitted before 1958, by which time the success of reconstruction was assured. By contrast (though the two cases are not totally comparable) during the process of transition of the Central and Eastern European economies, there was a rush to convertibility and to relaxation of capital controls. This liberal environment for trade and finance has not been notably successful in attracting capital to the reconstruction effort (from 1992–1994 foreign direct investment for the entire region was only about the same as foreign direct investment in Malaysia) and has produced the bizarre result that the Russia Federation is a significant net capital *exporter* (EBRD, 1995). All successful examples of the creation of modern industrial economies, from nineteenth century Germany (Gerschenkron, 1962) to the modern Republic of Korea (Amsden, 1989), have been associated which interventionist policies in both trade and finance. History suggests that a laissez-faire international regime may well hinder rather than help the process of transformation in Central and Eastern Europe (Eatwell *et al.*, 1995).

The importance of the theoretical framework which informs economic policy is also clear in the inter-war period experience. As Peter Temin (1989) has made clear, the Depression of the 1930s was a product both of the loss of international financial control (the UK unable to sustain the international system as it had done before the First World War, and the US unwilling to do so), and the fact that governments were convinced of the necessity of deflationary policies. They had no alternative theory which would lead them to act otherwise. Without a change of "theory" by governments, without a willingness to pursue growth-oriented policies, no formal structure of financial controls would deliver recovery in OECD countries. Without a change of policy to encourage higher growth in the North, the prospects for successful growth strategies in the South are seriously reduced. Developing countries, however, could question this legacy by adopting a pragmatic stance to financial liberalization, and by considering whether the benefits of financial liberalization outweigh its costs and help foster the goals of sustainable human development.

It took the experience of the Depression and of economic management during World War II to change the stagnationist theory which wrought such damage in the 1930s. In the same way, it is unlikely today that a significant reassertion of control over international financial structures is possible without an equally major change in priorities and analyses by major governments. Such changes have historically been associated with the aftermath of world-wide economic and political disruption.

Notes

1. "Speculative" trades may be made in hope of capital gain, or to hedge against potential capital loss, or to seek gains by arbitrage.

2. Keynes had the support of the United Kingdom Treasury and the Bank of England. Initially, Harry Dexter White and the US Treasury supported Keynes's position, but the American position was watered down under pressure from Wall Street (Helleiner, 1994).

3. Less careful writers simply assume what should be proved. For example, Blundell-Wignall and Browne (1991) begin an examination of the macroeconomic consequences of financial liberalization with the statement: ". . . it is a premise of this study that financial liberalization is an important step toward better-functioning market economies."

4. If no one can be made better off without someone else being made worse off, then an economy is said to have reached a state of Pareto optimality. Moreover, the so-called Third Theorem of Welfare economics demonstrates that there is no logically infallible way to aggregate the preferences of individuals and so to solve the problem of distribution. Allan Feldman (1987) sums up the state of welfare economics as: "We feel we know, as Adam Smith knew, which policies would increase the wealth of nations. But because of all our theoretical goblins, we can no longer prove it."

5. In circumstances in which decisions affect the path of the economy through time, the assumption of competitive markets that underpins the Fundamental Theorem must be supplemented by the rational expectations

hypothesis. Even so, there is no presumption that the competitive economy is stable. Not only might there be multiple equilibria (Obstfeld, 1986) but also there exists no general proof of the global stability of competitive equilibrium (Fisher, 1983). Taken by itself, the Efficient Markets Hypothesis embodies no presumption that the real economy is in a competitive equilibrium. It is a hypothesis about the use of information by financial markets, however that information may be generated.

6. These claims are spelt out in a recent survey of global financial markets and their policy implications (Woodall, 1995). They are the "conventional wisdom" on the subject. For example, Bayoumi and MacDonald (1995) also assert that "... open capital markets can provide the same services across countries that they provide within a single economy, allowing more efficient use of funds for investment and improving the allocation of consumption over time. These gains, which are similar to those accruing to individuals from capital markets within a country, were the logic behind the general move toward international financial liberalization since the late 1970s."

7. Woodall (1995) argues that ".. a government's loss of powers is reason to cheer, not fear: all that is being lost is the power to pursue damaging policies and practice economic deception by letting inflation rip."

8. An alternative approach to the Feldstein-Horioka result has been to investigate whether capital is sufficiently mobile to permit consumers to insulate themselves against national shocks, smoothing consumption and ensuring that consumption paths in individual countries are highly correlated with aggregate consumption across all countries. Although conclusions are less clear cut, there is little evidence of perfect capital mobility (Bayoumi and MacDonald, 1995).

9. The separation of British and German monetary policy following Britain's exit from the ERM in September 1992, is an example of currency risk in a fluctuating exchange rate system "insulating" interest rate differentials.

10. A deficit in the current account, whether of a country or region, must be matched by a net inflow of capital. The net inflow will be composed of direct investment and borrowing. In so far as borrowing predominates, the deficit region will tend to accumulate indebtedness, limiting the possibility of future deficits. Within nation states the accumulation of debt in

deficit regions tends to be mitigated by transfer payments (Commission of the European Communities, 1977).

11. As is well known, the ratio of debt to GDP will grow exponentially if the real rate of interest is greater than the real rate of growth. On the implications of this relationship for the US external debt, see Godley (1995).

12. This figure is an under-estimate, since it excludes UK data on foreign exchange forwards and swaps, as well as transactions between non-reporting entities. Including these trades would add around $7000 billion to the total (see BIS, 1996).

13. The same may be said of non-foreign exchange derivatives. Under the headline "Volatility is Making Hedges Grow," Suzanne McGee (1995) reported in the *Wall Street Journal* that "price uncertainty and market volatility are driving producers and consumers of energy products and metals to hedge their exposure in greater numbers than ever before. The result: Wall Street dealers are gleefully anticipating surging sales of commodity derivatives to these companies."

14. The collapse of Barings provides an excellent example of the challenges faced by the regulatory authorities. Prior to the collapse, Mr. Eddie George, the Governor of the Bank of England, wrote in *The Observer* of 24 July 1994, that

> "We now have an expert team monitoring derivatives who are getting even better every time they go in to see a firm. What they are reporting back from the most active players in the market is very reassuring. These people know what they are doing whether it's at director level or the chaps on the desk."

In a similar vein, Mr. Brian Quinn, the Bank of England director in charge of banking supervision, wrote in the *Bank of England Quarterly Bulletin* in August 1994 that

> "I believe both the market participants and the regulatory authorities have come a considerable way in identifying the capital needed for derivatives and all other instruments carrying market risk."

Yet the *Report* of the Board of Banking Supervision's enquiry into the Barings collapse concluded: "We believe the Bank should explore ways of increasing its understanding of the non-banking businesses (particularly financial services businesses) undertaken by those banking groups for which it is responsible..." (para 14.35).

"The Bank should ensure that it understands the key elements of the management and control structures of those banking groups where it is responsible for consolidated supervision" (para. 14.37).

15. Why this might happen is discussed in Section 3, below.

16. On this point, Mello and Parsons (1995) argue: "We think Culp and Miller play down the funding risk too much and lean far too much on the idea that Metallgesellschaft's creditors and shareholders should have readily coughed up extra cash. Culp and Miller have argued in the abstract that Metallgesellschaft *could not* have really faced a liquidity constraint, except as Deutsche Bank and others foolishly chose not to continue financing the oil business. ... Speaking of Deutsche Bank as if it had unlimited pockets is simply not facing up to the real-world constraints that had already been evidenced."

17. Derivatives such as commodity futures were originally developed to hedge environmental risks, such as harvest failures, rather than risks inherent in the operation of markets themselves.

18. The relationship between investment and growth is, of course, not simple. High rates of investment may be wasteful and may lead to a long-term slowdown in growth rates. But in this Report the accumulation of capacity is presumed to enhance the output and growth potential of the economy.

19. Ethiopia, Syria and Tanzania meet these criteria but are excluded from Table 5 because of lack of data. They are included in Table 7.

20. In the past three years, there has been a sharp fall in Japanese investment, virtually no growth in GDP, a sharp increase in unemployment, and a growing public-sector deficit.

21. The papers by Alesina, Grilli and Milesi-Ferretti (1994) and Grilli and Milesi-Ferretti (1995), referred to above, consider the relationship between a variety of institutional variables, including capital controls and economic performance. They find a positive, though weak, relationship between capital controls and growth of income per head. The relationship is strongest in the former paper, which studies 20 OECD countries over the period 1950–1989.

22. There is some disagreement about exactly what the beneficial impact of Black Wednesday consisted in. The most obvious point is that

the devaluation of a previously overvalued exchange rate improved the trade performance of the economy, and provided a stimulus to effective demand via increased net exports. But the increase in exports in 1993–94 was predominantly due to the growth of overseas markets, rather than any increase in competitive market share, and the share of imports in national expenditure actually increased (Eatwell, 1995a). Of far greater importance than the exchange rate effect was the relaxation of monetary policy which became possible once the uncertainty associated with the new floating rate regime permitted some de-coupling of British and German interest rates (Eatwell, 1994).

23. There was no speculation against the currencies of Austria, Belgium, or the Netherlands, countries for which the commitment to the maintenance of the parity with the Dmark was "credible" (Crockett, 1993).

24. There are, of course, other theories of inflation that would produce the same outcome. Those models that claim to identify a Non-Inflation Accelerating Rate of Unemployment (or NAIRU), determined by structural factors, and relate the acceleration to the level of effective demand, lead to conclusions similar to that derived from the natural rate hypothesis, even though the presumed behavioral mechanisms are different. There is for example no tendency for the economy to gravitate toward the NAIRU, and inflation is determined by the level of effective demand, not the rate of growth of the money supply (Rowthorn, 1977; Parkin, 1987).

25. In like manner, Tobin (1980) argues that "It is hard to resist or refute the suspicion that the operational NAIRU gravitates toward the average rate of unemployment actually experienced."

26. It is notable that the fiscal surpluses enjoyed by the British government in the late 1980s were associated that a sharp fall in the private-sector savings ratio. It could be argued that it was not government prudence which produced the surplus but the lack of prudence of the private sector.

27. Today, Keynesian theory is typically interpreted in terms of "rigidities" that inhibit the ability of markets to ensure a gravitation towards full employment equilibrium. In other words, an underemployment equilibrium is a special case of the full employment model, distinguished only by the imperfections (market failures) which prevent the attainment of Walrasian equilibrium. An alternative interpretation is that Keynes's vision is of an underemployment equilibrium determined by a level of effective demand that displays no tendency, even in the best of all possible worlds,

to gravitate toward full employment. This is not a special case of the neoclassical model, but an alternative to it. These issues are surveyed and analysed in Eatwell and Milgate, 1983.

28. The emphasis on "theory" in this sentence is perhaps excessive. The abandonment of the Bretton Woods system was not necessarily the preferred choice of most governments, but resulted from international financial developments that they were increasingly incapable of controlling.

29. A similar story might be told of the pound, which swung wildly from over $2.40 in 1980, to near $1.00 in 1986 to $2.00 in 1990, hardly a reflection of "fundamentals."

30. Another good example of the damage that imprudent financial flows can do is the large-scale bank lending to developing countries in the late 1970s, particularly to Latin America, which precipitated the debt crisis from which real output has barely recovered.

31. Exchange rate uncertainty drives a wedge between national interest rates, but the decoupling depends on the maintenance of uncertainty.

32. A study by Cho and Khatkhate (1989) of financial liberalization in five Asian countries (Indonesia, Malaysia, Philippines, South Korea and Sri Lanka), cited by Singh (1993), concluded: ". . . financial reform, whether comprehensive and sweeping or measured and gradual, does not seem to have made any significant difference to the saving and investment activities in liberalized economies. It was believed until recently that removal of repressive polices would boost saving. The survey in this paper of the consequences of reforms does not reveal any systematic trend or pattern in regard to saving (and also investment), though it clearly demonstrates that reform has greatly contributed to the financialization of savings." Devlin, Ffrench-Davis and Griffith-Jones (1995), commenting on the Latin American experience, 1991–1993, observe that "Mexico— although experiencing a particularly large influx of private capital—has not seen .. a recovery of growth in the period," and for Latin America as a whole, "national savings were crowded-out by external savings."

33. Singh and Hamid examine a sample of 50 of the largest manufacturing companies over the period 1980–1988 in each of nine countries: India, Jordan, Malaysia, Mexico, Pakistan, South Korea, Thailand, Turkey and Zimbabwe.

34. Singh (1993) cites the description in *The Economist* (9 September 1989) of the Taiwan stock market as "a rigid casino with a phenomenal

turnover." In 1989 the average value of shares traded on the Taipei stock market was nearly $3 billion, $1 billion more than in London, and just half the value of a day's trading in New York.

35. Schwert's finding (1989) that stock market volatility in the United States was high during the 1930s runs contrary to this image of a long-run stable depression. However, Bayoumi and Eichengreen (1994) find that "under fixed rates, monetary policy had to be adjusted to stabilize the exchange rate, flattening the demand curve and thereby increasing the output response and reducing the price response to aggregate supply shock. Following the shift to floating, monetary policy was freed, steepening the demand curve and increasing price volatility relative to output volatility."

36. These were, of course, the hypotheses that provided the theoretical underpinning of Keynes's position at the Bretton Woods conference.

37. This potential is acknowledged even by proponents of financial liberalization. For example, in rejecting the "Myth of the Powerless State," Pam Woodall (1995) argues that the "myth" was propped up by politicians unwilling to take public responsibility for their liberalizing decisions. "The world has changed, the global economy has indeed arrived: nonetheless, the emasculated state is a myth. . .The barriers that politicians have lowered can be raised again. . . In finance, technology makes the changes harder to reverse, but by no means impossible. . . given the will, governments can do it."

Bibliography

Akyüz, Yilmaz. and Andrew Cornford. (1994). *Regimes for International Capital Movements and Some Proposals for Reform*, UNCTAD Discussion Papers, no. 83.
Alesina, Alberto., Vitorio Grilli and Gian Maria Milesi-Ferretti. (1994). "The Political Economy of Capital Controls, in Leonardo Leiderman and Assaf Razin (eds.).
Amsden, Alice. (1989). *Asia's Next Giant: South Korea and Late Industrialisation*. Oxford: Oxford University Press.
Bank for International Settlements (BIS). (1992). *62nd Annual Report*, Basle.
_____ (1993). *Survey of Foreign Exchange Activity in April 1992*. Basle.
_____ (1995). *65th Annual Report*. Basle.
_____ (1996). *Central Bank Survey of Foreign Exchange and Derivatives Market Activity, 1995*. Basle.
Barro, Robert. (1974). "Are Government Bonds Net Wealth?," *Journal of Political Economy* 82(6): 1095–1117.
Bayoumi, Tamim. (1990). "Saving-investment Correlations: Immobile Capital, Government Policy, or Endogenous Behaviour," *IMF Staff Papers*. 37(2): 3360–387.
Bayoumi, Tamim, and Barry Eichengreen. (1994). "Macroeconomic Adjustment Under Bretton Woods and the Post-Bretton Woods Float: an impulse-response analysis," *Economic Journal* 104(425): 813–827.
Bayoumi, Tamim, and Ronald MacDonald. (1995). "Consumption, Income, and International Capital Market Integration," *IMF Staff Papers* 42(3): 552–576.

Bayoumi, Tamim, and Andrew Rose. (1992). "Domestic Savings and Intranational Capital Flows," *European Economic Review* 37(6): 1197–1202.
Baxter, Marianne, and Alan C. Stockman. (1989). "Business Cycles and the Exchange-Rate Regime: Some International Evidence," *Journal of Monetary Economics* 23(3): 377–400.
Black, Stanley W. (1987). "International Monetary Institutions," in John Eatwell, Murray Milgate and Peter Newman (eds.).
Blanchard, Olivier J. (1987). "Crowding Out," in John Eatwell, Murray Milgate and Peter Newman (eds.).
Blundell-Wignall, Adrian and Frank Browne. (1991). "Macroeconomic Consequences of Financial Liberalization: a Summary Report," *OECD Department of Economics and Statistics Working Papers*, no. 98.
Blundell-Wignall, Adrian, Frank Browne, and Paolo Manasse. (1990). "Monetary Policy in the Wake of Financial Liberalization," *OECD Department of Economics and Statistics Working Papers*, no. 77.
Bohm, Peter. (1987). "Second Best," in John Eatwell, Murray Milgate and Peter Newman (eds.).
Bordo, Michael. (1993). "The Bretton Woods International Monetary System: an Historical Overview," in Michael Bordo and Barry Eichengreen (eds.).
Bordo, Michael and Barry Eichengreen (eds.), (1993). *A Retrospective on the Bretton Woods System*, Chicago: University of Chicago Press.
Bryant, Ralph. (1987). *International Financial Intermediation*. Washington, DC: Brookings Institution.
Camdessus, Michel. (1994). "The Way Forward for the International Monetary System—50 Years after Bretton Woods," *IMF Survey*, May.
Cho, Yoon-Je, and Deena Khatkhate. (1989). "Financial Liberalization: Issues and Evidence," *Economic and Political Weekly*, 20th May.
Coakley, Jerry, Farida Kulasi and Ron Smith. (1995). "The Feldstein-Horioka Puzzle and Capital Mobility," *Birbeck College Discussion Papers in Economics*, no. 6/95.
Commission of the European Communities. (1977). *Report of the Study Group on the Role of Public Finance in European Integration*. Economic and Financial Series no. 13, volumes I and II. Luxembourg. (The MacDougall Report).
Corbett, Jenny and Tim Jenkinson. (1994). "The Financing of Industry 1970–89: an International Comparison," *Centre for Economic Policy Research, Discussion Paper, no. 948*. London.

Crockett, Andrew. (1984). "Exchange Rate Volatility and World Trade," *IMF Occasional Paper, no. 28*. Washington, D.C.

Crockett, Andrew. (1993). "Monetary Policy Implications of Increased Capital Flows," in Federal Reserve Bank of Kansas City. *Symposium*.

Culp, Christopher and Merton Miller. (1995). "Metallgesellschaft and the Economics of Synthetic Storage," *Journal of Applied Corporate Finance* 7(4): 62–76.

De Grauwe, Paul. (1987). "International Monetary Policy," in John Eatwell, Murray Milgate and Peter Newman (eds.).

Devlin, Robert, Ricardo Ffrench-Davis and Stephany Griffith-Jones. (1995). "Surges in Capital Flows and Development: an Overview of Policy Issues in the Nineties," in Ricardo Ffrench-Davis and Stephany Griffith-Jones (eds.), *Coping with Capital Surges: the Return of Finance to Latin America*. Boulder and London: Lynne Reinner.

Dornbusch, Rudiger. (1976). "Expectations and Exchange Rate Dynamics," *Journal of Political Economy* 84(6): 1161–1176.

Eatwell, John. (1994). "The Coordination of Macro-economic Policy in the European Community," in John Grieve Smith and Jonathan Michie (eds.), *Unemployment in Europe*, London: Academic Press.

Eatwell, John. (1995a). "A Recovery Faltering Through Lack of Investment," *The Observer*, 27 August.

Eatwell, John. (1995b). "Disguised Unemployment: the G7 Experience," *UNCTAD Review*: 67–90.

Eatwell, John. (1996). "Unemployment on a World Scale," in John Eatwell (ed.), *Global Unemployment: Loss of Jobs in the '90s*. Armonk, New York: M.E. Sharpe.

Eatwell, John, Michael Ellman, Metz Karlsson, D. Mario Nuti and Judith Shapiro, (1995). *Transformation and Integration: Shaping the Future of Central and Eastern Europe*. London: IPPR.

Eatwell, John, and Murray Milgate (eds.). (1983). *Keynes's Economics and the Theory of Value and Distribution*. London: Duckworth.

Eatwell, John, Murray Milgate and Peter Newman (eds.), (1987). *The New Palgrave: A Dictionary of Economics*. London: Macmillan.

Edey, Malcolm, and Ketil Hviding. (1995). "An Assessment of Financial Reform in OECD Countries," *OECD Economics Department Working Papers*, no. 154.

Edwards, Franklin. (1993). "Financial Markets in Transition—or the Decline of Commercial Banking," in Federal Reserve Bank of Kansas City, *Symposium*.

Eichengreen, Barry (1993). "Epilogue," in Michael Bordo and Barry Eichengreen (eds.).

European Bank for Reconstruction and Development (EBRD). (1995). *Transition Report Update*. London.

Fazzari, Stephen, R. Glenn Hubbard and Bruce Petersen. (1988). "Financing Constraints and Corporate Investment," *Brookings Papers on Economic Activity* 1: 141–195.

Federal Reserve Bank of Kansas City. (1988). *Financial Market Volatility. A Symposium*.

Federal Reserve Bank of Kansas City. (1993). *Changing Capital Markets: Implications for Monetary Policy. A Symposium*.

Feldman, Allan. (1987). "Welfare Economics," in John Eatwell, Murray Milgate and Peter Newman (eds.).

Feldstein, Martin. (1994). "Tax Policy and International Capital Flows," *Weltwirtschaftliches Archiv* 11130(4): 675–697.

Feldstein, Martin and Philippe Bacchetta. (1991). "National Saving and International Investment," in John Shoven and Douglas Bernheim (eds.), *The Economics of Saving*. Chicago: University of Chicago Press.

Feldstein, Martin and Charles Horioka. (1980). "Domestic Saving and International Capital Flows," *Economic Journal* 90(358): 314–329.

Felix, David. (1995). "Financial Globalization versus Free Trade: the Case for the Tobin Tax," *UNCTAD Discussion Papers*, no. 108.

Fisher, Franklin. (1983). *Disequilibrium Foundations of Equilibrium Economics*, Cambridge: Cambridge University Press.

Frank, Julian and Colin Mayer. (1990). "Capital Markets and Corporate Control: a Study of France, Germany and the United Kingdom," *Economic Policy* 5(10): 189–231.

Frankel, Jeffrey A. (1992). "Measuring International Capital Mobility: a Review," *American Economic Review* 82(2): 197–202.

Friedman, Milton. (1968). "The Role of Monetary Policy," *American Economic Review* 58(1): 1–17.

Gagnon, Joseph E. (1993). "Exchange Rate Variability and the Level of International Trade," *Journal of International Economics* 34(3–4): 269–287.

Gertler, Mark, and R. Glenn Hubbard (1988). "Financial Factors in Business Fluctuations," in Federal Reserve Bank of Kansas City, *Symposium*.

Gerschenkron, Alexander. (1962). *Economic Backwardness in Historical Perspective*. Cambridge, Mass.: Harvard University Press.

Giovanetti, Giorgia. (1991). "Exchange Rate Volatility, Prices and Trade Flows," *Revue d'Economie Industrielle*.

Godley, Wynne. (1995). "A Critical Imbalance in US Trade: the US Balance of Payments, International Indebtedness, and Economic Policy," *The Jerome Levy Economics Institute Public Policy Brief*, no. 23.

Goldberg, Linda S. (1993). "Exchange Rates and Investment in United States Industry," *Review of Economics and Statistics* 75(4): 575–558.

Gordon, David. (1987). "Six-percent Unemployment Ain't Natural: Demystifying the Idea of a Rising 'Natural Rate of Unemployment,'" *Social Research* 54(2): 223–246.

Graaff, Jan de Villiers. (1957). *Theoretical Welfare Economics*. Cambridge: Cambridge University Press.

Grilli, Vittorio and Gian Maria Milesi-Ferretti. (1995). "Economic Effects and Structural Determinants of Capital Controls," *IMF Staff Papers*, 42(3): 517–551.

Helleiner, Eric. (1994). *States and the Re-Emergence of Global Finance: from Bretton Woods to the 1990s*. Ithaca: Cornell University Press.

Homer, Sidney and Richard Sylla. (1991). *A History of Interest Rates*. New Brunswick, New Jersey: Rutgers University Press.

Huizinga, John. (1994). "Exchange Rate Volatility, Uncertainty, and Investment," in Leonardo Leiderman and Assaf Razin (eds.).

Kalecki, Michael. (1937). "The Principle of Increasing Risk," *Economica*.

Keating, Giles, and Jonathan Wilmot. (1992). *Prosperity or Decline*. London: Credit Suisse First Boston.

Keohane, Robert O., and Helen V. Milner (eds.). (1996). *Internationalization and Domestic Policies*. Cambridge: Cambridge University Press.

Keynes, John Maynard. (1933). "National Self-sufficiency," *New Statesman and Nation*, 8th and 15th July; as reprinted in *The Collected Writings of J.M. Keynes*, volume XXI. Macmillan, London, 1982.

Keynes, John Maynard. (1936). *The General Theory of Employment, Interest and Money*, London: Macmillan.

King, Mervyn. (1995). "Credibility and Monetary Policy," *Scottish Journal of Political Economy* 42(1): 1–19.

King, Mervyn and Sunil Wadhwani. (1988). "Transmission of Volatility between Stock Markets," *LSE Financial Markets Group Working Papers*, no. 48, London School of Economics.

Krugman, Paul. (1993). "Comment" on Marston (1993), in Michael Bordo and Barry Eichengreen (eds.).

Leiderman Leonardo and Assaf Razin (eds.). (1994). *Capital Mobility: The Impact on Consumption, Investment and Growth*. Cambridge: Cambridge University Press.

Lipsey, Richard and Kelvin Lancaster, (1956). "The General Theory of Second Best," *Review of Economic Studies* 24(1): 11–32.

McGee, Susan. (1995). "Volatility is Making Hedges Grow," *Wall Street Journal*, 12 June.

Malkiel, Burton. (1987). "Efficient Market Hypothesis," in John Eatwell, Murray Milgate and Peter Newman (eds.).

Marston, Richard. (1993). "Interest Differentials under Bretton Woods and the Post-Bretton Woods Float: the Effects of Capital Controls and Exchange Risk," in Michael Bordo and Barry Eichengreen (eds.).

Mello, Antonio and John Parsons. (1995). "Maturity Structure of a Hedge Matters: Lessons from the Metallgesellschaft Debacle," *Journal of Applied Corporate Finance* 8(1): 106–120.

Mussa, Michael and Morris Goldstein. (1993). "The Integration of World Capital Markets," in Federal Reserve Bank of Kansas City, *Symposium*.

Naples, Michele and Arben Arifaj. (1995). "Measuring Business Failures for Policy Purposes: the 1983–84 Data Discontinuity and Creation of a Consistent Series," *mimeo*, Trenton State College, New Jersey.

Obstfeld, Maurice (1986). "Rational and Self-fulfilling Balance of Payments Crises," *American Economic Review* 76(1): 72–81.

Obstfeld, Maurice (1993). "International Capital Mobility in the 1990s," *NBER Working Paper*, no. 4534.

Orr, Adrian, Malcom Edey and Michael Kennedy. (1995). "The Determinants of Real Long term Interest Rates," *OECD Department of Economics and Statistics Working Papers*, no. 155.

Parkin, Michael. (1987). "Inflation," in John Eatwell, Murray Milgate and Peter Newman (eds.).

Phelps, Edmund. (1967). "Money Wage Dynamics and Labour Market Equilibrium," *Journal of Political Economy* 76(4): 678–711.

Pollin, Robert. (1995). "Financial Structures and Egalitarian Economic Policy," *New Left Review* 214: 26–61.

Rowthorn, Robert. (1977). "Conflict, Inflation and Money," *Cambridge Journal of Economics* 1(3): 215–239.

Schwert, G. William. (1989). "Why does Stock Market Volatility Change Over Time," *Journal of Finance* 44(5): 1115–1153.

Shiller, Robert. (1988). "Causes of Changing Financial Market Volatility," in Federal Reserve Bank of Kansas City, *Symposium*.

Singh, Ajit. (1993). "The Stock Market and Economic Development: Should Developing Countries Encourage Stock Markets?," *UNCTAD Review*: 1–28.

Singh, Ajit. (1994). "Openness and the Market-friendly Approach to Development: Learning the Right Lessons from Development Experience," *World Development* 22(16): 1811–1823.

Singh, Ajit. (1995). "Pension Reform, the Stock Market, Capital Formation and Economic Growth: a Critical Commentary on the World Bank's Proposals," *mimeo*, Cambridge.

Singh, Ajit and Javed Hamid. (1992). *Corporate Financial Structures in Developing Countries*. Washington DC: IFC Technical Paper, no.1, World Bank.

Sinn, Stefan. (1992). "Saving-investment Correlations and Capital Mobility," *Economic Journal* 102(414): 1162–1170.

Solow, Robert M. (1990). *The Labour Market as a Social Institution*, Oxford: Blackwell.

Sudweeks, Bryan L. (1989). *Equity Market Development in Developing Countries*. New York: Praeger.

Taylor, Lance and Jonathan Schlefer. (1995). "Mexico's Made-in-USA Mess," *Washington Post*, 8th October.

Temin, Peter (1989). *Lessons from the Great Depression*. Cambridge, Mass.: MIT Press.

Triffin, Robert. (1960). *Gold and the Dollar Crisis*. New Haven: Yale University Press.

United Nations (UN). (1993). *World Economic Survey, 1993*. New York: United Nations.

United Nations (UN). (1995). *World Economic and Social Survey. 1995*. New York: United Nations.

Woodall, Pamela. (1995). "The World Economy: Financial Markets, a Survey," *The Economist*, 7 October.

World Bank. (1994). *Averting the Old Age Crisis: Policies to Protect the Old and Promote Growth*. New York: Oxford University Press.

World Institute for Development Economics Research (WIDER). (1990) *Foreign Portfolio Investment in Emerging Equity Markets*. Helsinki: United Nations.

Author's Biographical Note

John Eatwell is a Fellow of Trinity College, Cambridge, England, and a Professor of Economics at the New School for Social Research, New York. In January 1997, he becomes the President of Queens' College, Cambridge. He is the author of numerous books and articles on economics and economic policy. Amongst his books are *An Introduction to Modern Economics* (1973), *Keynes's Economics and the Theory of Value and Distribution* (1983), *Transformation and Integration: Shaping the Future of Central and Eastern Europe* (1995), and *Global Unemployment: loss of jobs in the '90s* (1996).

He was a co-editor, with Murray Milgate and Peter Newman, of *The New Palgrave: A Dictionary of Economics*, 4 volumes (1987), which was listed by *The Times Literary Supplement* of 6 October 1995 as one of the "hundred most influential books published since the war." He was also co-editor of *The New Palgrave Dictionary of Money and Finance* (1992).